THE ROAD

TEN STEPS TO AUTHENTIC MINISTRY

AHEAD

FOR INDEPENDENT BAPTISTS

PAUL CHAPPELL

First published in 2013 by Striving Together Publications, a
ministry of Lancaster Baptist Church, Lancaster, CA 93535.
Striving Together Publications is committed to providing
tried, trusted, and proven books that will further equip local
churches to carry out the Great Commission. Your comments
and suggestions are valued.

Striving Together Publications
4020 E. Lancaster Blvd.
Lancaster, CA 93535
800.201.7748

Cover design by Andrew Jones
Layout by Craig Parker
Edited by Monica Bass
Special thanks to our proofreaders

The author and publication team have put forth every effort to give
proper credit to quotes and thoughts that are not original with the
author. It is not our intent to claim originality with any quote or
thought that could not readily be tied to an original source.

ISBN 978-1-59894-237-8

Printed in the United States of America

Dedication

To my sons, Larry and Matt Chappell. May God
use you mightily on the road ahead.

Dr. Paul Chappell has challenged independent Baptists to answer David's question to his brothers, "Is there not a cause?" We must agree that the cause is not about us…it is about Jesus and bringing honor and glory to His name. It is about reaching a lost world with the gospel of Jesus Christ!

DR. RICK ADAMS, PORTLAND, OREGON

I believe Paul Chappell has helped younger pastors who are tempted to throw out the baby with the bath water and older pastors who want to keep the baby in the dirty water.

DR. JEFFREY AMSBAUGH, JOHNSTON, RHODE ISLAND

In a day when those who hold to the truth are mocking the truth, this book is a timely breath of fresh air to those wishing to have a balanced ministry of truth and grace. Thank you, Pastor Chappell, for addressing the "elephant in the room" that cannot be ignored any longer.

MISSIONARY JOHN ANDERSON, LONDON, ENGLAND

This book clearly addresses the issues we face in a loving, direct, and helpful manner. The Road Ahead *will become a primer for Bible college students and a manual for all of us.*

PASTOR BRENT ARMSTRONG, TUCSON, ARIZONA

In every generation there are Goliaths that loom larger than life and threaten the impact and viability of a church, several churches, or even a movement. If we fail to address and slay the giant in our generation, the "giant" issues remain for the next generation to tackle. In this poignant book, Dr. Chappell has graciously taken on some of the modern day Goliath issues among independent Baptists and provides a balanced approach to positioning churches to more effectively fulfill the Great Commission for such a time as this.

DR. ROBERT BAKSS, ROCKHAMPTON, AUSTRALIA

This book deals with crucial issues all of us encounter, but the approach is biblical, relevant, and practical.

DR. KENNY BALDWIN, BAILEY'S CROSSROADS, VIRGINIA

Dr. Chappell has written a much needed book. His perspectives and insights are biblically grounded.

EVANGELIST BENNY BECKUM, STATESBORO, GEORGIA

This book will help us find the balance we need to stay out of the ditches of judgmental, pharisaical legalism on the one side and judgmental, contemporary, anything goes on the other.

EVANGELIST BUDDY BLUNKALL, HOT SPRINGS, ARKANSAS

This is a book whose time has come. While independent Baptists have typically stood in the right position, our disposition has often betrayed us. Pastor Chappell has openly, honestly, and gracefully dealt with internal issues that have "blackened the eye" and hindered the progress of our ranks. The transparency and purity of this dialogue is refreshing.

PASTOR TIM BUTLER, GREENVILLE, NORTH CAROLINA

This book serves as a wake-up call to Baptists of what is worth defending and what is not. It shows how we as Bible-preaching Baptists arrived where we are, and it provides a road map of what must be done if we don't wish to lose the next generation of pastors. A great conversation starter, this book should be a must read for all pastors, young and old alike, who sincerely desire to earnestly contend for the faith in the twenty-first century.

PASTOR TROY CALVERT, FAIRFAX STATION, VIRGINIA

A must read for anyone who calls himself a fundamental independent Baptist. With the brilliance of a carefully guided scalpel, Dr. Chappell carefully and humbly walks us through issues that have been looming in fundamental independent Baptist circles for a long time. By the grace of God and for His glory, Dr. Chappell gives us clarity and hope for our biblical Baptist churches in a day of compromise and apostasy.

DR. BUD CALVERT, LAKELAND, FLORIDA

What a joy to have a book that takes an honest and bold look at the independent Baptist condition. It is much harder to do a checkup than an autopsy, but to be healthy again, it is a necessity. Thank you for your transparency in helping preachers and individuals to not only remember their heritage but to biblically show us how to have a glorious future.

PASTOR DAVID CASHMAN, FAIRLESS HILLS, PENNSYLVANIA

What an equipping book! Thank you for this challenge to pastors to approach current issues from a biblical perspective and to serve God's people with biblical balance. The book itself is a model of balancing grace and truth.

PASTOR STEPHEN CHAPPELL, OCEANSIDE, CALIFORNIA

Wise, thought-provoking, biblical steps for us Baptists on the road ahead. I highly recommend this timely book.

PASTOR CHARLIE CLARK, BERLIN, NEW JERSEY

I believe The Road Ahead *is a needed book at this juncture of our Baptist movement. Pastor Chappell has brought into the light the heartfelt sentiments of many of his fellow pastors. We are frustrated with the tangents, the imbalances, and the caustic nature of some of our brethren. I am greatly burdened for our young people who are becoming cynical and jaded by the inconsistent actions they witness on a regular basis. We have to be willing to face realities, address them, and correct them or turn away from them. Thank you, Brother Chappell, for being willing to open up this discussion that is so long overdue.*

PASTOR GORDON CONNER, VANCOUVER, BRITISH COLUMBIA

May we take these thoughts to heart and allow God to shine His light through our ministries in the coming generations. God bless you for a God-given concern and a right spirit among biblical Baptists.

PASTOR MIKE CREED, CLINTON, MARYLAND

Boldly authentic. Significantly timely. A must read for every pastor who is tired and frustrated with so many inconsistencies but who loves our heritage.

PASTOR DAVE DELANEY, LOUISVILLE, KENTUCKY

The Road Ahead *requires that we honestly appraise the path we are on. God has greatly blessed the bold positions independent Baptists have taken for decades. Moving forward, however, we must take care that our separatist positions remain on the foundation of biblical principles. When we become followers of men and places, we run the risk of dividing ourselves over traditions and preferences that ultimately hurt the cause of Christ. This book brilliantly speaks to this vital issue of our day.*

PASTOR MICHAEL EDWARDS, WOODBRIDGE, VIRGINIA

Dr. Paul Chappell's new book The Road Ahead *is a must read for any concerned fundamental Baptist. The substance and spirit of this book is helpful and encouraging.*

DR. TOM FARRELL, TAYLORS, SOUTH CAROLINA

Brother Chappell has again brought us wise counsel for the challenges that face God's people in the battle. I pray the Lord will use his new book to help us all formulate policies that glorify our Father in Heaven and safeguard the ministries with which we have been charged. May God again revive His people so the world may again see the light of His glory and grace!

DR. RICHARD FLANDERS, VASSAR, MICHIGAN

As a seasoned pastor, watching some young men depart from our historic Baptist positions has been disheartening. This book addressed the issue head on. It confronts both sides with truth that needs to be stated. It causes us to re-examine our positions to make sure they are firmly rooted in truth—but it is also expressed with grace. I commend Brother Chappell for taking on this important task that no doubt will help many preachers.

DR. KEVIN FOLGER, CLEVELAND, OHIO

I highly recommend this book as a must read for every pastor, deacon, and Sunday school teacher of an independent fundamental Baptist church. This book will help clarify and reaffirm the biblical standard and right spirit of an independent fundamental Baptist pastor and church. Pastor Chappell has made a great contribution for the cause of Christ.

PASTOR ALAN FONG, SAN LEANDRO, CALIFORNIA

Reading this book encouraged me to continue to do the things that make a true New Testament local church, to preach and teach the Word of God without compromise but with compassion, and to maintain a proper ministry balance. I honestly think that this is a must read for every man who pastors or feels called to pastor a local New Testament church.

DR. FRANK GAGLIANO, SPRINGFIELD, TENNESSEE

The Road Ahead *is an insightful look at where the fundamental, independent Baptist movement has come from and where it is moving. The heart of this book comes through in a clear way we must side on biblical truth as strong as ever. But it reminds us that we must do it with a disposition that will exemplify the love of Christ. A wonderful read that encouraged me in my stand for the faith of the gospel.*

PASTOR JOHN GOETSCH, JR., YUMA, ARIZONA

Whenever I've had the opportunity to be with Pastor Chappell, either in his church or in his home, I always come away spiritually challenged and encouraged in two areas: The first is that Pastor Chappell is a fervent soulwinner, and he is constantly imparting his passion for reaching the lost to those around him. The second area is his servant leadership. Even though Pastor Chappell leads a large ministry, he is a loving servant to his Lord, to his wife and family, and to everyone he meets. He practices what he preaches. Dr. Chappell tries to communicate his heart in The Road Ahead, *and he does so in a masterful way. Read it and heed it. May God bless our churches with revival as we strive to reach our world for Christ.*

DR. RON HAMILTON, GREENVILLE, SOUTH CAROLINA

I gladly recommend The Road Ahead *because it makes a biblical, heartfelt appeal to spiritual leaders for unity—which is the hope for revival for our nation.*

DR. RAYMOND HANCOCK, HAMPTON, GEORGIA

One guiding principle that has helped me in recent years is expressed in the phrase, "There is a ditch on both sides of the road." In trying to avoid falling into the ditch "over there," independent Baptists have slid into their own. Brother Chappell skillfully articulates ditches that are seriously undermining our progress. America needs the very best that independent Baptists have to offer. The challenge presented by Brother Chappell in The Road Ahead *is absolutely necessary to churches that intend to be part of the solution instead of part of the problem.*

PASTOR WAYNE HARDY, STILLWATER, OKLAHOMA

I highly recommend this helpful book that not only honestly deals with a serious problem in fundamentalism today, but provides biblical solutions to some of our most pressing issues.

EVANGELIST HAL HIGHTOWER, LEBANON, MICHIGAN

Every once in a while a book is written that has the potential to have an exponential impact on generations to come. Dr. Paul Chappell's The Road Ahead *is one such book. The biblically balanced strategy laid out within the pages of this book deserves to be heard and heeded by both younger and older pastors alike.*

PASTOR JOSH IRMLER, FRESNO, CALIFORNIA

The Road Ahead *is just what we have been waiting for! Pastors and spiritual leaders from every generation, whether seasoned or just beginning in ministry, will glean solid biblical principles.*

PASTOR RYAN JOHNSON, REDWOOD CITY, CALIFORNIA

I am convinced that our dear Lord guided Paul Chappell to accurately describe "the last days" quandary of relevance facing independent, fundamental Baptists. The Road Ahead *is a must read for each Baptist preacher seriously desiring to rightly divide the word of truth (2 Timothy 2:15), earnestly contend for the faith (Jude 3), take the "high road" in brotherly controversies (Romans 14:10), and finish his course with biblical convictions (2 Timothy 4:7). I most highly recommend this book without reservation.*

DR. J. C. JOINER, TUCSON, ARIZONA

I appreciate the insight and courage of Dr. Chappell in pointing out the high cost of our infighting. Our problem does not lie in our doctrine—that has not changed—but in the shortage of the Spirit of Christ within the body of Christ. The very existence of The Road Ahead *is evidence we are identifying our problem and willing to deal with it.*

DR. CHARLES KEEN, MILFORD, OHIO

We'll never know how needed this book was until the day we stand before the Lord. This book clearly put forth balanced ministry for independent Baptist churches, as is written in Ephesians 4:11–15.

DR. DANIEL KIM, SEOUL, SOUTH KOREA

I have been an independent Baptist pastor for over twenty-five years. I wish I could have read a book like this in those early days. It would have saved me much fear, worry, and insecurity. Thank you, Pastor Chappell, for having a heart for the next generation of preachers.

PASTOR CURTIS KING, HAGERSTOWN, MARYLAND

The Road Ahead *brilliantly identifies the "identity crisis" that has occurred among our independent Baptist churches. It presents us with an accurate and encouraging glance at our rich heritage in the past, a candid and hopeful viewpoint on our present, and a solid, biblical strategy for our future. This book is a must read for every serious Christian desiring to present and represent Christ clearly and compassionately to a skeptical and misled world.*

DR. PAUL KINGSBURY, ROCKFORD, ILLINOIS

Sometimes Christians find themselves with different opinions regarding ministry philosophy and standards. Dr. Paul Chappell takes this issue biblically with grace and gives good answers to younger and older preachers as well as other believers.

DR. HWANGRO LEE, PATERSON, NEW JERSEY

This is the book for the hour. Dr. Paul Chappell takes us on a journey from our past heritage and biblical foundation to our present condition with a wonderful spirit of grace and concern. I was deeply moved as I read through these pages and saw in print the wonderful heritage we have as Baptists. I also see the problems that we are encountering in our present day and was blessed by Dr. Chappell's compassionate approach to dealing with these issues. Every pastor should get a copy of this book and read it. I know that I will use what I have learned to be the biblical Baptist pastor I should be.

PASTOR RON LEVERSEE, GILBERT, ARIZONA

This book addresses those issues that many have been unwilling to confront for the danger of being misquoted or misrepresented. Paul Chappell does not shy away from the potential risks; but boldly, definitively, graciously, and, most importantly, biblically, presents the great dilemmas in our movement at this time. This book could be the catalyst —the "gamechanger"—for the independent Baptist movement in coming generations.

DR. SHANE LEWIS, SOMERVILLE, ALABAMA

Finally, we have a proactive approach to ministry as independent Baptists. If you are passionate about living out your Christianity biblically and with balance, the principles outlined in this book will be of great help to you.

PASTOR NATHAN LLOYD, BRISBANE, AUSTRALIA

This book will make you think. It brings answers to difficult questions based on Scripture by a man who has a love for pastors and a passion to honor God in everything he does. Knowing him personally for many years and seeing his integrity makes me appreciate this book even more.

DR. RICK MARTIN, ILOILO CITY, PHILIPPINES

What a great resource book! The Road Ahead is a well-written, easy-read book and should be in the library of anyone serious about ministry. Dr. Chappell vividly portrays where we've come from and expertly charts a course for advancing the cause of Christ in this twenty-first century. Once I started reading, I couldn't put it down.

DR. DAVID MCCOY, MCDONOUGH, GEORGIA

An honest look at the issues of independent Baptists. I believe this book will help us to keep our eyes on Jesus!

DR. GERALD MCKELROY, WACO, TEXAS

A fresh call to all pastors, young and old, this book helps us remember the history and heritage of Baptists. We will be challenged not to run from our name, but to return to our purpose.

PASTOR KERRY NANCE, TAMPA, FLORIDA

The Road Ahead gives clear insight to the dangerous direction of many churches today. It will assist preachers in hitting the reset button without changing the distinctives of the New Testament Baptist church.

DR. DEAN NOONAN, OAK CREEK, WISCONSIN

Dr. Chappell's book accurately assesses our movement and gives timely advice as to how we can effectively define ourselves in this pagan culture. I trust you will prayerfully read these pages with an open heart, then ask God how you can effectively reach this generation of the lost.

DR. MIKE NORRIS, MURFREESBORO, TENNESSEE

An eye-opener, this is a must read for both pastors and members of local churches.

PASTOR LARRY OBERO, NATIONAL CITY, CALIFORNIA

The Road Ahead *assesses our condition as Bible-believing Baptists with unusual clarity, addresses burdens of ministry with unfailing compassion, and maintains our biblical position with unabashed conviction. It bridges generational differences and provides a clear scriptural path for the future.*

DR. R. B. OUELLETTE, BRIDGEPORT, MICHIGAN

Being a first-generation Christian and a first-generation independent Baptist, this book has helped me understand our Baptist heritage.

DR. LUIS PARADA, LONG BEACH, CALIFORNIA

The honesty with which the book is written will help any reader to aptly navigate "the road ahead."

PASTOR TIM RABON, RALEIGH, NORTH CAROLINA

A clear, thought-provoking book regarding "the road ahead" for independent fundamental Baptists and why our identity is fast becoming more cultural than biblical. A must read!

PASTOR TERRY RANDOLPH, PHOENIX, ARIZONA

Could hardly put it down! This is a must read for veterans and young preachers alike, written by a seasoned, experienced pastor of pastors. Enjoy! Be helped! Gain insight! Be blessed!

PASTOR MIKE RAY, NAPA, CALIFORNIA

The Road Ahead *is written with a spirit that should mark all the followers of Christ—grace and truth. No matter what "camp" in which you consider yourself to be, you should camp here for awhile!*

DR. JEFF REDLIN, FORT COLLINS, COLORADO

Timely, informative, and courageous. Dr. Chappell has explored for us new territory which pastors desirous of reaching the lost and preaching God's Word unapologetically must consider in the culture in which we minister.

DR. DAN REED, ACWORTH, GEORGIA

The Road Ahead *is a call to all of us who identify as independent Baptists. It is a call to assessment and an encouragement to be sure we are pursuing the objective of having a biblically balanced ministry.*

PASTOR BILL RENCH, TEMECULA, CALIFORNIA

It is an honor to recommend this book. I believe it will help enlighten younger and older pastors and that it will help us examine our ministries to make certain we are utilizing every opportunity available as we meet the challenges facing our churches and members. It encourages us to commit what time we have left to serve the Lord and lead our people in a way that would please Him, help Christians grow and mature, and reach the lost.

DR. BOBBY ROBERSON, WALKERTOWN, NORTH CAROLINA

My prayer is that the Lord will use this book mightily to bring revival to our country. May the Lord help us lead by example as we reflect the image of our Lord and Saviour. Thank you for your heart and concern for the cause of Christ and the gospel.

DR. EZEKIEL SALAZAR, LOS ANGELES, CALIFORNIA

A must read for the pastor who wants to develop authentic, Bible-based ministry. Pastor Chappell accurately articulates our strengths and our challenges.

PASTOR ERIK SANDERS, EVERETT, WASHINGTON

Dr. Chappell has captured in essence the biblical breath that has long been lost in Baptist circles.

PASTOR S. C. SCHEARER, GREAT FALLS, MONTANA

Thank you for having the courage and wisdom to stand with God's Word and against unbiblical practices and attitudes in ministry! This book is a must read for anyone desiring to serve God with a biblical philosophy of ministry.

PASTOR CARY SCHMIDT, NEWINGTON, CONNECTICUT

It is an honor to heartily endorse and recommend The Road Ahead. *Pastor Chappell has masterfully blended his discerning observations of the landscape of fundamental Baptists with solutions that are biblical and workable. He has walked a delicate tightrope with a gracious and impressive combination of compassion, conviction, and courage. May our Saviour use this book to call us back to the business of the Great Commission.*

EVANGELIST PAUL SCHWANKE, DESERT HILLS, ARIZONA

I found this book to be clear, accurate, and helpful. The insight to Baptist history, philosophy, and practice is on point. I pray this book will be received with the spirit in which it was written.

PASTOR STAN SMITH, SAN JOSE, CALIFORNIA

A much needed book describing the past, present, and future of the independent Baptist movement. Dr. Chappell suggests using the term biblical Baptist to describe our movement in light of all the negative reporting by the secular and even religious media. I highly recommend this book.

DR. DAVID SORENSON, DULUTH, MINNESOTA

Dr. Chappell addressed the issues of our movement in a style that gives direction and purpose for the next generation. This content is a stabilizer in a world of compromise and change. These instructions come from a leader who has lived his life around the great fundamental leaders of the past and has seen the transition of today. A tremendous read for anyone who seriously loves the work of the ministry and its future.

PASTOR RICK STONESTREET, FAIRFIELD, CALIFORNIA

Being isolated in Hawaii, we learned the necessity of crossing "party lines" for fellowship and cooperation. I am thankful for the thoughtful and heartfelt challenge for each of us to practice grace and to find strength in our unity despite our differences. Thank you, Dr. Chappell, for having the courage and grace to write it.

PASTOR WAYNE SURFACE, HONOLULU, HAWAII

I believe this book will be a great help to Bible-believing Baptists. I thank God for the insight that He has given to Pastor Chappell. The balance between autonomy and fellowship is well stated.

PASTOR DAVE TEIS, LAS VEGAS, NEVADA

Of all the Striving Together Publications resources, I would have to place The Road Ahead *at the very top. This book will be a breath of fresh air for any young pastor connected with the independent Baptist movement.*

PASTOR JOSH TEIS, LAS VEGAS, NEVADA

I applaud the courage and willingness to tackle such a tough, controversial topic with the desire to help honest preachers and leaders who wish to be biblical in approach and stand while not being caught up in the division mentioned in this book. It will be a help to sincere people who want to be faithful to our Baptist distinctives, loyal to God's Word, and effective in a lost and dying world.

PASTOR RANDY TEWELL, THEODORE, ALABAMA

Throughout church history, God has used men to shape and form the future. They were visionary and even revolutionary. Paul Chappell is such a man, and The Road Ahead *is such a book. It is a must read for everyone who loves the local church and the independent Baptist movement.*

PASTOR DWIGHT TOMLINSON, NEWPORT BEACH, CALIFORNIA

With honesty and yet a passion for the local church, Dr. Chappell addresses the important reality of the church's present perception versus her reality. This book will challenge you to be thoughtful and purposeful while genuine in reaching this world with the gospel, as well as passing on to the next generation the faith "once delivered to the saints."

DR. ROBERT WALL, AJAX, ONTARIO

Very frank and written in a Christlike spirit. An encouragement for biblical unity in reaching a lost world.

DR. WILLIE WEAVER, FORTH WORTH, TEXAS

If you are looking to grow deep roots which will result in a fruitful ministry, this is the book. The Road Ahead *is exactly what pastors and Christian leaders need to read today. Biblical and balanced! This is a book I am giving to all of our "Timothys" in the ministry.*

PASTOR SCOTT WENDAL, COLLEGEVILLE, PENNSYLVANIA

Acknowledgements

Many men across America have discussed and prayed with me about these truths. I appreciate their interest and input. The men whom shared a recommendation on the previous pages read through the manuscript and made comments for which I am grateful.

I also greatly appreciate the input from men on our church pastoral staff as well as the administrative and Bible faculty of West Coast Baptist College. It is a privilege to labor with these men in the work of the Lord.

Larry Chappell	Dr. John Goetsch	Dr. Don Sisk
Tim Christoson	Rick Houk	Gary Spaeth
Jerry Ferrso	Dane Keely	Dr. Toby Weaver
Enoch Kim	Dr. Mike Lester	Reggie Williams
Carlos Navarrete	Dr. Mark Rasmussen	Dr. Mike Zachary
Tobi England	Bryan Samms	
Dr. Jerry Goddard	Dr. Jim Schettler	

Contents

FOREWORD › xxi

PREFACE › xxv

STEP ONE › Understand the Problem of a Tarnished Name   1

STEP TWO › Remain Steadfast to the Truth   11

STEP THREE › Remember Our Heritage   21

STEP FOUR › Enjoy Biblical Fellowship   45

STEP FIVE › Confront False Teaching and Sin   55

STEP SIX › Correct Imbalance in Ministry   69

STEP SEVEN › Be Grace Givers   99

STEP EIGHT › Engage Younger Pastors in Ministry Conversation   133

STEP NINE › Return to Soulwinning and Outreach   151

STEP TEN › Identify Ourselves Biblically and Wisely   165

CONCLUSION › 179

EPILOGUE › 185

APPENDIX 1 › On the Late Massacre in Piedmont   187

APPENDIX 2 › Ten Marks of Imbalance in Ministry   189

APPENDIX 3 › Instructions for American Servicemen
in Britain, 1942   193

APPENDIX 4 › Concerns and Hopes for Preachers   197

APPENDIX 5 › Sample Policies for Local Church Ministries   203

SCRIPTURE INDEX › 221

Foreword

B Y THE TIME YOU TURN eighty, you've had the opportunity to learn much by simple observation. In the past fifty-five years of ministry, I've had the privilege to both observe and know many dear servants of the Lord. God has used so many of them to touch my life, and I trust I have been able to encourage them as well.

One of these men whom I've been blessed to serve with is Dr. Paul Chappell. For the past twenty years, I have had the opportunity to work with him in a variety of ministries. These opportunities, as well as our personal friendship, have given me an inside vantage point from which to observe his life. I'd like to tell you what I've seen.

I have watched as Pastor Chappell has faced tremendous trials. Through each of these trials, I have been thrilled to see him manifest a greater faith and determination to be all that God would have him be.

I've watched as the Lancaster Baptist Church and West Coast Baptist College have grown. Behind the scenes, I've noticed a significantly growing passion in the heart of Paul Chappell to be used of God. I've noticed a magnified sense in his heart of his total dependence on the Lord.

I've watched—and listened—as Dr. Chappell has shared in personal conversations his great desire to be a blessing and a help to pastors and to local churches around the nation. I've watched him give of himself in ways that most will never know as he seeks to encourage, edify, and befriend in any way that he can. I've even observed him desire to be a friend and a help to those who have criticized him or tried to hurt him in some way. His desire to help these men is real, and it is a mark of gracious humility.

I've watched as Pastor Chappell and the Lancaster Baptist Church invest hundreds of thousands of dollars and untold manpower hours into the annual Spiritual Leadership Conference. From a business angle, the meeting is a liability and an exhausting use of energy. But for Pastor Chappell, the meeting is an opportunity to provide help and encouragement to Christian workers around the world.

Why do I tell you these traits I've observed in Dr. Chappell? To give you an understanding of the driving purpose behind the book you hold in your hands. Every word in these pages was written with the simple desire to be a help—to you.

And these words are needed as well!

We serve the Lord in unprecedented days. The truths which we hold dear are under assault from every side. On one hand, they are being eroded by an unbelieving world, but on the other hand, they are being abused by those who preach them but do not practice them.

To give you perspective of where I'm coming from, I began my ministry in 1956 pastoring churches in a Baptist convention. Before long, I became concerned about their theological trends toward liberalism. I was grieved when I understood they were hiring theologically liberal professors in their colleges and seminaries and supporting and sending missionaries who questioned the inerrancy of Scripture through their cooperative program. In 1963, I left the convention.

For over fifty years now, it has been my delight to be an independent Baptist and to serve in and plant independent Baptist churches. I have preached in independent Baptist churches all across America and in more than sixty countries around the world. I love the name *Baptist,* and I believe in the independence—or autonomy—of the local New Testament church.

I am disturbed and saddened when young pastors become disillusioned with our movement because of the actions and attitudes of some within our ranks. But in all honesty, I can understand their frustration. If independent Baptist churches are to have the impact on our nation and in unreached nations around the world, we must work together—we must choose truth-based unity. We must once again focus our attention on the Lord and the needs of a lost world.

As I reviewed *The Road Ahead,* I found the candor and transparency to be so fresh that it seemed as if I were sitting with Pastor Chappell discussing the issues independent Baptists face today. He wrote with a heart of love balanced with the firmness of a biblical position.

The Road Ahead was a breath of fresh air to me, and I believe it will be to you a long, heart-to-heart conversation with a good friend. Allow me to encourage you to carve out a few hours and let Pastor Chappell speak to you as your friend through these pages.

Dr. Don Sisk
Missions Department Chairman, West Coast Baptist College
President Emeritus, Baptist International Missions Incorporated

Preface

IF YOU BELIEVE THE NAME of Christ and the name *Christian* is worthy of our best and is more important than any other title, you may be interested in this book.

If you are a Baptist who is thankful for the courageous stand of martyrs for the faith and the heritage of truth left by our forefathers, you may be interested in this book.

If you believe it is important to admit that imbalances have existed among some churches and pastors who identify themselves as conservative or fundamental and that the next generation of preachers is helped when we admit our own shortcomings, you may be interested in this book.

If you believe you can emphasize a holy lifestyle with a loving spirit, you may be interested in this book.

If you believe that being independent means no other pastor, college, magazine, or parachurch organization speaks for you, you may be interested in this book.

If you believe that division over slight, non-biblical issues have relegated a once strong movement of soulwinning churches to a divided and often irrelevant voice in America, you may be interested in this book.

If you hold to the conviction of an autonomous local church and to fundamental Bible doctrines, but have not historically referred to yourself with the expression "IFB," you may be interested in this book.

If you believe that grace is not a license to sin, but that grace does teach us to live a godly lifestyle with kindness toward our brethren, you may be interested in this book.

If you believe it is time to say goodbye to the caustic bloggers, hateful preachers, and fruitless commentators and to get back to winning souls and being faithful to the Word, you may be interested in this book.

If you believe God is still able to bring revival to repentant hearts and that there is hope for America, you may be interested in this book.

This book is written by a friend and co-laborer in the midst of the work. Each page comes to you from a pastor who deeply loves the work of the Lord, loves his family, and delights to care for and serve the Lord with His people.

In these pages, we face some broad and prickly topics. I've done my best to organize them into succinct chapters, and for your sake, I've made an effort not to be redundant where there is an overlap of relativity between chapters. I suggest, however, that to gain a thorough understanding of this material, you commit to a complete read-through of the book.

It is my prayer that this book will prompt us to examine our hearts, renew our passion for the Great Commission, and—most of all—bring glory to Jesus Christ, whose churches we are privileged to serve.

Understand the Problem of a Tarnished Name

"**S**O YOU ARE AN AMERICAN?"

Before I had time to respond to the heavily accented question at the airport in Seoul, my new-found friend continued, "You must be like President Obama!"

How do you tell someone whose English is limited that yes, you're an American…and thrilled and thankful to be one. But, no, you're not the same kind of American as the international face of your country?

It's kind of awkward.

To me, being an American means I believe in liberty and freedom and that I enjoy the opportunity to express these.

But to foreigners whose paradigm of my country is shaped by Hollywood and liberal politicians, being an American conjures up an entirely dissimilar image. I always want to quantify what an American really is.

I am an American—as patriotic as they come! But not like *that*.

More and more, I find myself in a similar predicament in relation to the name "independent fundamental Baptist." I am one—through and through! But not like some.

Let me explain.

MY JOURNEY

When you think about it, it's almost humorous that we Baptists use the expression "I'm Baptist born and Baptist bred." Technically, none of us believe that anyone was "Baptist born" since no one is a true Baptist who hasn't made a personal decision to trust Christ. Nonetheless, if you *could* be Baptist born, I was. And since you can't be, I became a Baptist immediately after my salvation!

Not only was I an immediate Baptist, but I was an immediate independent fundamental Baptist. The oldest son of an independent Baptist pastor, I grew up during one of the most exciting periods of the movement. Being an independent fundamental Baptist in the 1960s and 70s was exciting. Elmer Towns published *The Ten Largest Sunday Schools in America* in 1969, and we occupied a majority of the spots. People were being saved, and churches were growing exponentially through aggressive soulwinning and outreach.

Even as a boy, I had the opportunity to know some of the outstanding leaders of our movement. My fifth grade Sunday school teacher gave me a leather-bound Bible, and I immediately began filling the front and back blank pages with the signatures of guest pastors and preachers—many of whom spent time as guests in our home. I respected and admired these men and their ministries. Although some shifted in philosophies over the years, I still have that Bible, and it contains the autographs of such men as John R. Rice, G. B. Vick, B. Myron Cedarholm, Tom Malone, Jack Hyles, Curtis Hutson, Lester Roloff, Lee Roberson, C. W. Fisk, Jerry Falwell, Jack Garner, Jim Lyons, Jack Baskin, W. E. Dowell, Monroe Parker, and many more.

Later, as a pastor, I had some of these same men and many other independent Baptists in the pulpit of Lancaster Baptist Church.

Additionally, the Lord has given me opportunity to preach for and with many leaders within the independent Baptist movement. I have shared platforms with men such as Tom Malone, A. V. Henderson, Rod Bell, Clarence Sexton, Jack Hyles, Lee Roberson, Frank Bumpus, Wayne Van Gelderen, Curtis Hutson, Jack Baskin, Tom Farrell, Sam Davison, Raymond Hancock, Jack Trieber, Roy Thompson, Shelton Smith, Rick Martin, Dave Hardy, Lou Baldwin, Bobby Roberson, and Don Sisk.

Across the nation, I have had opportunity to preach for the Baptist Bible Fellowship, the Fundamental Baptist Fellowship, the Southwide Baptist Fellowship, the Nationwide Independent Baptist Fellowship, the Global Independent Baptist Fellowship, the Hammond Pastors' School, and the national Sword of the Lord Conference.

All that to say, I have known and been blessed by the leadership and fellowship of many men and wonderful people in independent Baptist churches. This movement has been a part of my life since day one, and even before I began ministry as a nineteen-year-old, I knew that I was an independent fundamental Baptist by conviction. (I'll explain these convictions in chapter 2.)

I will always be thankful for my early heritage. God allowed me to be influenced by courageous men who were staunch in their faith and committed to truth. Most of these men had separated from denominations or conventions where inerrancy was questioned, doctrine was weakened, and holiness was ignored. These were men of backbone, and as I began my own ministry, I was thankful to stand in their ranks.

Looking back, some of the influences in my life through this movement were not as grace-based or Christlike in their ministry philosophy and practice as Scripture indicates we should be. Unfortunately, I followed some of their tendencies in my own leadership style for the first few years of ministry until the Lord began to teach me some vital lessons regarding a spirit of biblical grace and how it was a missing element in my own ministry. God led me patiently and, at times, painfully away from philosophies that were more fleshly than spiritual.[1]

> I will always be thankful for my early heritage.

In my personal journey, I came to a definite place of decision when as a young pastor I learned that one of my early mentors had failed morally. I cried myself to sleep every night for several days following. While I was still reeling from the shock, I learned that this was not the first time he had failed, that previously he had been helped to "move on" to another ministry.

To say that I was shaken would be an understatement. On a personal level, I was devastated. But even beyond the personal loss, I was deeply disturbed with how this sin had been handled.

---

1   Much of this I shared in the book *Guided by Grace*, Sword of the Lord Publishers, 2000.

I began to question my heritage, my doctrinal moorings, and my ministry affiliations. God manifested His grace in my life through an abundance of means during this season. He gathered me in His arms and comforted me. At the same time, He refocused my gaze off the leadership of men and onto Him alone.

It was actually through this experience that I first began to truly appreciate the biblical strengths of the independent Baptists while recognizing the fallibility of men. I became less naïve but, by God's grace, more committed to the principles and practices of biblical, New Testament local church ministry. God taught me to move from His Word forward in a causative fashion, rather than reacting from issue to issue along the way.

Frankly, I'm still on a journey to learn servant leadership and Christlikeness. In my own life and in our ministry, there's continuing growth and adjustment as we strive for a balance that honors and glorifies the Lord.

REACTIONS AND RESPONSES

Proverbs 22:1 tells us "A good name is rather to be chosen than great riches." Although I have given much of my life to strengthening pastors and churches within the independent Baptist ranks, I have, along with many others, been burdened for the testimony of our biblical heritage because of the actions and attitudes of some.

As we will see in future chapters, every group has its weaknesses. Some of those weaknesses are inherent to the unbiblical practices of the group, but most are inherent to the humanity of leaders in general. Simply put, leaders from every group or denomination fail.

In fact, one of the concerning trends I see among younger leaders is that of holding leaders within and without our ranks to different levels of expectation. The same pastors who turn from the philosophies of their earlier mentors will give a "pass" to leaders of other movements, holding them to lower expectations while claiming they are more spiritual. For instance, a young leader may reject a mentor because of his persistently angry spirit. But he is not always so quick to write off leaders within another group for the same fault. We ought to be holding all spiritual leaders to the same standard to which we hold those who have disappointed us.

If you are a spiritual leader who is considering your personal stand or "place" in ministry, let me encourage you for a moment. In our nation alone, there are approximately fourteen thousand independent Baptist churches.[2] Some of them have behaved unscripturally or have not led spiritually. But there are many thousands more who are true to Christ, faithful in soulwinning and discipleship, and nurturing Christian growth in the context of a healthy ministry philosophy. I personally know hundreds of pastors who are godly men who love their families and are spiritual servant leaders in their churches.

> Simply put, leaders from every group or denomination fail.

In a recent conversation with Dr. Richard Flanders, he likewise shared the testimony of biblical Baptists he's known over the past decades as being men of integrity. He mentioned, "These pastors have *historically* been characterized by humility, self-sacrifice, ethics, commitment to principle, godliness, careful Bible preaching,

---

2   *Church Still Works* (Striving Together Publications, 2009), 14–15.

and personal holiness for many years." What he says is true, and it is important that we retain an accurate perspective when we are inclined to broad brush many with the caricature of a few.

Through the years, I have seen many pastors become disillusioned or discouraged when a mentor falls. And I can empathize. I've been there, and it's painful. Just because a strong leader sins, however, does not mean we discard truth or principle. We should not allow our reaction to drive us away from biblical responses. I've seen pastors radically change their entire ministry philosophy in a reaction to the failure of a mentor. It is as if they are saying, "Whatever 'he' emphasized, I'm turning from." Many of these men who have made the choice to abandon the philosophies they had once practiced weren't grounded in their doctrinal position in the first place—their positional moorings were tied to a leader rather than to Christ.

A LARGER PICTURE

Beyond our personal responses and journeys, I believe we have come to a serious place nationally. Because of the unscriptural attitudes and actions of some, and because we live in a day when bloggers and the media can exploit these, in some instances our name has become tarnished.[3]

Whereas identifying yourself as an independent Baptist traditionally was a statement of believing historic Baptist doctrine and functioning independently of a denomination, this

---

3   For a more thorough treatment of this subject, see the article "A Clean Name or a New Name?" Available at http://www.paulchappell. com/2011/04/27/a-clean-name-or-a-new-name/.

identification is often not so much about doctrine or practice anymore. Sadly, all too often in these days, some "independent fundamental Baptist" churches are known for a mix of the following:

- Mishandling sinful issues
- Pastors being unapproachable and living without accountability (immunity within leadership)
- Recommending immoral pastors to other churches
- Angry pulpits
- Petty divisions over beliefs that are not scripturally supported
- Excessive loyalty to a personality or institution
- A Christianity focused more on externals than the heart
- Strange child discipline
- Not properly reporting abuse
- Insecure, authoritarian, and prideful leadership
- Rules instead of relationships
- Emphasis on the fear of man more than on the fear of God
- Outward appearance over inward transformation

While the majority of independent Baptist churches are Christ-honoring and have godly leadership, it seems like an unbalanced few, assisted exponentially by technology, have sent a sad, "name damaging" message that is cast upon the whole.

Frankly, the media would consider all truly biblical ministries from any denomination "weird." But, however peculiar the lost may deem us to be, they should see integrity and godliness in our churches. In his book, *The Integrity Crisis*, Warren Wiersbe wrote, "The Church has grown accustomed to hearing people question the *message* of the gospel, because that message is foolishness to the lost. But today the situation is embarrassingly reversed, for now the *messenger* is suspect."[4]

TARNISHED SPLENDOR

So what do we do when a name becomes tarnished?

I believe it's time for revival in our midst. It's time for a name cleansing. It's time for some to move from:

- Bully pulpits with straw man issues back to authentic Bible preaching and teaching
- The wrath of man to speaking the truth in love
- Mishandling sin to handling sin with integrity and biblical principle
- Paranoid isolation (for pastors/church members) to loving engagement with family, neighbors, and the community
- Petty preferences to personal holiness
- Excuse-making to church building
- Critical spirits to edification and encouragement

For many years, I have taught that we must define the meaning of terms to a suspicious culture. Now, more than ever before, it's time we do a better job at defining ourselves than those who "say all manner of evil…falsely" (Matthew 5:11).

Since the first century, Christians have had detractors, and spiritual leaders have often been misunderstood and

---

4   Warren W. Wiersbe, *The Integrity Crisis* (Oliver-Nelson books, a division of Thomas Nelson, Inc., Publishers, 1988), 17.

misrepresented. The world will always hate the name of Christ, and it will always attack His messengers (John 15:18–21). And yet, we need to be clear in who we are and what are our intentions. Those to whom we seek to minister should not have to wonder about our integrity, accountability, or purity.

You and I have the privilege to bear the name of Christ as we serve. We carry the name that is above every name—*Jesus*. He is why we should be concerned with any name that is a reflection on His church.

There is no doubt in my mind that our society and media will become more hateful toward biblically based Baptist ministries in the days ahead, and I believe it's important that we position ourselves biblically and rightly in this generation.

In the coming pages, I invite you to look at some of the weaknesses and inconsistencies within our movement that have been hurtful to the cause of Christ. And I invite you to a frank discussion regarding the steps each of us can take to reclaim authentic ministry and seek greater revival.

Thank you for caring enough to read. It is my prayer that you will read prayerfully. Let us pray together for a renewed testimony and for revival in our midst.

> Let your light so shine before men, that they may see your good works, and glorify your Father which is in heaven.—MATTHEW 5:16

Remain Steadfast
to the Truth

O NCE A YEAR, I WALK through the sterile doors of Scripps Clinic in San Diego. The deacons of our church are firm in their resolve that I do so. I'm thankful that our deacons care about my health enough to insist that I annually schedule a physical checkup and evaluation. These appointments typically result in some adjustment of lifestyle and/or medication.

Many of the most common life-threatening diseases of our day are best nabbed if detected in their earliest stages. Tragically, many times we get so busy running through life that we fail to take time for needed evaluation and mid-course adjustments.

We not only need annual *physical* evaluations, but we also need regular *spiritual* and even *ministry* evaluations. To remain spiritually healthy and firmly grounded in truth, we periodically need to step back and make time for a checkup.

I pray that this book proves to be that sort of a checkup. Before we delve into some of the more serious issues, however, I want to be sure that we are on the same page. Although we will examine ministry practices and heart attitudes, this book is not about abandoning truth or uplifting a spirit of pragmatism.

Most independent Baptist churches are doctrinally sound in that their founding documents and statements of faith clearly speak to their conviction for the orthodox truth which was once delivered to the saints (Jude 3). My doctrinal convictions have been clearly stated for thirty years. I've preached them from the pulpit of Lancaster Baptist Church, placed them on multiple websites, and articulated them in conferences around the country for nearly three decades.

This book will not denigrate the heritage of preachers who have held to scriptural truths, planted churches, and paved the way for men like myself in ministry. We owe far more than we even know to the courageous Baptist preachers of the past.

And yet, although I'm firm in my doctrinal position and deeply respect my fundamental heritage, I do believe the time has come for careful examination of the terms we use to describe our churches.

TRUTH AND LABELS

I have always liked using terms or labels to describe my position— not because I derive security from the labels—but because I believe that people deserve to know where our church stands.

For example, the word *Christian* has deep meaning to me. It refers to the first century when those who had chosen to follow Christ modeled a lifestyle that was so consistent with their faith that the unsaved identified them as followers of Christ—Christians (Acts 11:26).

Similarly, I am a *Baptist* by conviction. Although the name was given to us by our enemies (who originally called us "Anabaptist"),[1] the historic beliefs of Baptists have caused the name to be more than a descriptive word. To me, the word *Baptist* embodies my biblical position. When someone in our community sees our sign "Lancaster Baptist Church," they probably have at least a vague idea that we preach the Bible and that we have a different doctrinal statement than the Charismatic, Lutheran, or Catholic churches in town.

Additional terms I've used for most of my life are *independent* and *fundamental*. Accurate as these terms are of what I believe and practice, in the minds of some their meaning is becoming blurred. Of course, *independent* refers to the scriptural teaching of the autonomy of the local church, and *fundamental* refers to the orthodoxy of my faith. It seems, however, that the behavior and spirit of many who have identified themselves with the same terms I have used is becoming misleading.

Just as when I travel overseas I want to be sure people in other countries understand that I do not espouse the American "ideals" of President Obama—such as same-sex marriage, abortion, etc.— so now I'm finding myself in an increasingly difficult position when those who are not independent Baptist—saved and unsaved alike—ask about my affiliations. When people who do not have a historically shaped context of my chosen identification ask if I am an "independent fundamental Baptist," I often must distance

---

1   J.S. Hartzler and D. Kauffman, *Mennonite Church History* (Mennonite Book and Tract Society, 1905), 68.

myself from nationally known sins, inconsistencies, and caustic attitudes of some independent fundamental Baptists.

I recognize that a few of my friends may not like that last sentence. But most of my pastor friends understand exactly what I'm saying. They, like me, also see a host of solid younger men in our movement who are stepping onto the field of ministry and wondering if they want to be saddled with the challenging distraction of this identity baggage for the rest of their lives.

If you share my concerns, I want to encourage you to reaffirm your commitment to stand strong for truth, even if it means you must adjust or more clearly define your position.

CLARIFY THE TARGET

Later, we will discuss our options concerning labels. But we first must understand that, as important as labels are, the truth that they represent is far more important.

For the past twenty years or so, those who would market the church and encourage leaders to be "seeker driven" have been dispensing with and re-coining terminology to appeal to the modern man. These churches, led by entrepreneurial pastors, have sought to please men to the point that they have dropped the use of biblical terms (including such words as *justification, sanctification,* and *propitiation*), have not confronted "seekers" with a need for repentance, and often will not speak against the sins of our day.

Those who market the church to the culture tend to shed labels, so much so that they don't really tell you what they believe. Not only is this practice misleading, it is deceptive. The marketing pastors operate on the fear of man and the fear of society's perception.

Hence, they have dropped the use of even biblical terms such as *church, preaching, Hell, repentance, atonement,* and scores of others.

If you begin making terminology changes from the faulty position of the fear of man, you will one day realize that people of all kinds hate you anyway simply because you are a "Christian" who believes in the infallibility of a "Bible." The world has never been and never will be a friend to followers of Christ. For instance, in an April 2013 US military training briefing on extremism, an instructor listed "Evangelical Christianity" at the top of a slide listing "Religious Extremism." Other organizations listed included Catholicism, Al Qaeda, Hamas, the Ku Klux Klan, Sunni Muslims, and the Nation of Islam.[2]

> I want to encourage you to reaffirm your commitment to stand strong for truth.

When it comes to biblical truth, the discussion is far larger than terminology. If your goal in terminology choices is to be liked, accepted, and understood by the world, you must realize they reject Christ Himself—not just the terms you use. What will you do then? Become "emergent"? Explain away the faith? Or maybe leave the faith? I know of more than one previously "fundamental pastor" who has made these changes. If we need anything today, it is a move back to biblical terms, not away from them!

To the extent that the world or even ecumenical religion despises the name independent Baptist because of our doctrinal position, we must be willing to endure that hardship. If we are

2   Todd Starnes, FOX News & Commentary, "Army Labeled Evangelicals as Religious Extremists," April 5, 2013, http://radio.foxnews.com/toddstarnes/top-stories/army-labeled-evangelicals-as-religious-extremism.html.

primarily concerned about our label identity because of the fear of man's opinion, we may drift farther from the truth than we realize.

This book is not about accommodating theology.[3] I have no intent to adapt or compromise God's eternal truths because of our post-modern culture or even because some men in my own movement have tainted a good name.

I understand that many pastors in their twenties and thirties struggle with being "lumped in" with the troubling idiosyncrasies created by others. Conversely, I have friends who sometimes have a tendency to identify all "fundamental truth" as though it appeared shortly after 1950. Somehow they have missed out on the origination of the terms and the history that shaped them. In consequence, they have often failed to help others realize that these fundamental truths derive strictly from the first century, God-given, Holy Spirit-inspired Scripture. These good men spent too much of their ministries trying to get people to conform to a culture (often a '50s-ish culture) rather than to Christ. (I, too, spent time in this pastoral pursuit of conformity to a religious culture rather than conformity to Christ.) It is entirely possible to "look good" and conform to the culture of your group and still be a leader with a carnal heart.

In our defense, I'd hasten to add that I believe the hearts of these pastors have been sincere in that we believe in and seek to elevate the holiness of God. But too often the target of our ministry has also been to please a man or a college or a fellowship somewhere. With their acceptance in mind, we view our ministry

---

3   See *The Saviour Sensitive Church* for more thoughts on understanding and avoiding the seeker-sensitive church movement. Striving Together Publications, 2004.

through how the size of our church would look or be perceived by those we wanted to please. Hence our sin has sometimes been the same as that of the seeker church pastor; we just had a different—but equally wrong—target.

The only worthy goal or target in ministry is to exalt Jesus. Most maturing, growing pastors will go through enough trials and scriptural growth to purify their motives and clarify their goals. My goal is Christ. As I have said for years, success is a moving target, but leadership has a fixed goal, and my goal is Jesus.

A CROSSROADS ON THE PATH OF TRUTH

As we face the issues of divisiveness, a tarnished name, and, in some places, loss of soulwinning and church planting fervor, there are often a variety of responses from pastors and leaders.

1. Some accept the status quo. There are pastors who—either because they are toward the end of ministry and are too tired to consider the issues, or because they are happy to remain in their comfort zone—would prefer to continue on as they are. Some will be perturbed that I would bring these issues up for examination.

2. Some are turning from heritage and position. These pastors, particularly younger pastors, frustrated with the errors and inconsistencies in our group have chosen to follow Christian leaders from other groups—leaders who publicly drink, are open to modern-day tongues and promote non-cessationist views (that the miraculous, first-century sign gifts of the Holy Spirit continue today), and often have a hostile, condescending attitude toward ministries more conservative than their own.

3. Some are willing to ask the Holy Spirit to make a thorough examination and to send revival. This response is my personal desire. I choose to hold solid doctrine, treasure my biblical heritage, and honestly admit where imbalances have existed, seeking to correct mine and helping others do the same. This was the heart of the Apostle Paul, and he expressed it eloquently in Philippians 3:13–14, "Brethren, I count not myself to have apprehended: but this one thing I do, forgetting those things which are behind, and reaching forth unto those things which are before, I press toward the mark for the prize of the high calling of God in Christ Jesus."

I pray that this book will encourage those who have been leaning to the first or second choices above to consider this third option. Rather than getting annoyed or fleeing, I pray that we will ask the Holy Spirit to do a thorough cleansing in our lives and among our churches.

A CALL FOR AUTHENTIC REVIVAL

I write out of deep respect for many of my mentors who have run well doctrinally and morally—men who have fought the good fight of faith and set a godly example. I have spent much time and energy seeking out the faithful, balanced, aged men in our movement and honoring their examples. We are commanded scripturally to show them "double honor" (1 Timothy 5:17).

Additionally, I write with a genuine concern for younger pastors. I want to urge them to stay with truth. I want to converse with them as they reject the eccentricity and shortcomings they clearly see so that they avoid the man-pleasing philosophies or doctrinal errors that are offered as alternatives in other movements.

I write, primarily, with a passionate heart for my Lord. He is worthy of all glory in His church. When labels are for the sole purpose of group identity, we miss the focal point of the ministry—Jesus Himself.

If you are a young pastor who longs to see Jesus lifted up and glorified in the context of authentic, local church ministry that is true to the biblical model; if you are an older pastor who longs to see independent Baptist churches return to a Christ-ward focus that is centered around principles rather than personalities or places; if you are a pastor or leader of any age who wants to pour your life into what Jesus loved—the New Testament local church—and see it flourish and grow, then I share your heart.

This book is a call to personal godliness and biblical revival. It is a plea to Baptist pastors and spiritual leaders that we return to the scriptural model of servant leadership with focused evangelism and discipleship. It's a cry to turn from whatever glory we may perceive in our positions and standards and redirect it to focus every beam of glory on God and on God alone. May we step by step return to the authentic ministry path of biblical holiness, principle, and Spirit-anointed revival.

Are you up for the steps ahead? Let's start a ways back…

Remember Our Heritage

STOOPING INTO A CAVE WHERE persecuted Christians worshiped has a way of stripping your perspective down to the true essentials.

Last summer, I had the opportunity to visit the valleys of Piedmont, Italy, where thousands of Waldensians "kept the faith" in the harshest of conditions. Our guide led us to one of the caves where these Christians would meet secretly to sing hymns, pray together, and hear God's Word preached. As I stood in the damp stillness, I could picture twelfth-century Christians—probably about sixty at a time—huddled together in a common love for Jesus.

When we consider our heritage as Baptists and the saints who willingly paid a price for the faith hundreds of years before the Reformation, it is humbling—convicting. It speaks to the value of truth.

In the seventeenth century, the Waldensians of Italy paid a considerably high price for the truth. Their sacrifice is known today as the Massacre of Piedmont.

In April of 1655, the Duke of Savoy sent an army to the upper valleys in Italy that were inhabited by the Waldensians and ordered a gruesome slaughter. On Saturday, April 24, 1655, at 4:00 AM, the signal was given for a general massacre.

The horrors of this massacre are indescribable. Not content to simply kill their victims, the soldiers and monks who accompanied them invented barbaric tortures. Babies and children had limbs ripped off their bodies by sheer strength. Parents were forced to watch their children tortured to death before they themselves were tortured and killed. Fathers, forced to wear the decapitated heads of their own children, were marched to their death. Some of these Christians were literally plowed into their own fields. Some were flayed or burned alive. Many endured worse. Unburied bodies—dead and alive—covered the ground.

Hundreds of the Waldensians fled to a large cave in the towering Mount Castelluzzo. The murderous soldiers, however, tracked them there and hurled them down the precipice to their death. This is the reference in Milton's famous sonnet to "the bloody Piedmontese that rolled Mother with infant down the rocks."[1]

Survivors of this massacre were few, but they rallied together and wrote to Christians in Europe, pleading for help. Among these letters were the heart-rending words, "Our tears are no longer of water; they are of blood; they do not merely obscure our sight, they choke our very hearts."[2]

---

1   See Appendix 1 for complete sonnet.
2   J. A. Wylie, *The History of Protestantism, Vol. II*, 1878 (republished by Mourne Missionary Trust, Kilkeel, Northern Ireland, 1985), 486.

As I learned this story, it spoke to me on two counts. First, because we have not suffered much for the faith here in America, I'm afraid we don't value it as we should. Yet, the gospel that frees us and the Bible that has made it known to us have been loved and held dear by many who gave their lives rather than compromise their faith. Even today, in repressive nations around the world there are Christians faithfully and loyally suffering for Christ—some giving their lives.

Second, because we face little that could be called real persecution, we too easily get distracted from proclaiming the gospel. While Christians in other countries strengthen each other in the face of torture, we split hairs over the pettiest issues.

Something about the massacre in Piedmont helps put Christianity into perspective. It reminds us how valuable the faith is and how shallow our own faithfulness is. It reproves us for investing our time, energy, and loyalty into anything less than proclaiming the infallible Word of God and the gospel of Jesus Christ.

> Because we have not suffered much for the faith here in America, I'm afraid we don't value it as we should.

In the next few pages, I invite you to take a brief look at an overview of our Baptist heritage. As we skim over past centuries, notice that it is *truth* that survives—not movements, personalities, or ministry philosophies. Truth—concerning God's plan of salvation and concerning the local New Testament church—is what is essential to the propagation of the faith.

Let's take a brief look at the defining and distinctive beliefs that Baptists and their forefathers have held.

BAPTIST DISTINCTIVES

Many pastors use an acrostic of the word *Baptists* to highlight the distinctive doctrines of Baptists.[3]

Biblical authority
Autonomy of the local church
Priesthood of the believer
Two offices—pastor and deacon
Individual soul liberty
Separation of church and state
Two ordinances—baptism and the Lord's Table
Separation and personal holiness

While these phrases do not encompass every fundamental tenant of the faith, they do highlight those beliefs that distinguish us from other groups—Catholics, Reformed churches (Lutheran, Presbyterian, etc.), Charismatics, and others. Historically, no group other than Baptists holds *all* of these beliefs.

Biblical authority in all matters of faith and practice—We believe the Bible is inspired and infallible and is the final authority. It is from God's Word that we understand and teach the fundamental

---

3   I am aware that there are slight differences in this acrostic. For instance, some use the "P" to represent "Priority on regenerate membership" and an "S" to represent "Soul Liberty" or "Saved and baptized church membership." Whatever your preferences for this acrostic, in the end, it's not a statement of faith, but a tool for expressing distinctive beliefs. We could actually add several more letters!

doctrines of our faith as well as pattern our church polity. (See 2 Timothy 3:16; John 17:17; Acts 17:11; Hebrews 4:12; 2 Peter 1:20–21.)

Autonomy or self-governing power of the local church— We believe that every local church should be independent of a hierarchical framework or outside governmental structure. (See Colossians 1:18; Acts 13–14, 20:19–30; Ephesians 1:22–23.)

Priesthood of believers—God's Word assures believers that we have direct access to God through our relationship with Christ. We believe and teach that the priesthood of the believer is the unspeakably precious privilege of every child of God. (See Hebrews 4:14–16; 1 Timothy 2:5–6; 1 Peter 2:5–10.)

Two offices within the church—Scripture only mentions two church offices—pastor (also referred to as elder or bishop) and deacon. These two offices are to be filled by godly men of integrity in each local church. (See Philippians 1:1; Acts 6:1–7; 1 Timothy 3:1–13; Titus 1:6–9; 1 Peter 5:1–4.)

Individual soul liberty—We believe that each person must make a personal decision of repentance and faith in Christ. (See Romans 10:9–17, 14:1–23.)

Separation of church and state—The state should have no power to intervene in the free expression of religious liberty. (See Matthew 22:21; Acts 5:29–31; Romans 13:1–4.)

Two ordinances—baptism and the Lord's Table (also called communion)—These ordinances have no part in salvation and only serve as pictures of what Christ did for us. (See Matthew 28:19; 1 Corinthians 11:23–26; Acts 2:38–43, 8:36–38; Romans 6:1–6.)

Separation and personal holiness—We believe that Christ's ultimate sacrifice demands our complete consecration, and we desire that our daily living would reflect the holiness of our great God. (See 2 Corinthians 6:14; 1 Peter 1:16.)

Again, this acrostic is not exhaustive—nor is it meant to be. But it does represent core truths for which millions have given their lives. In fact, we can see these beliefs held in local churches from the time of the first century.

EARLY BEGINNINGS

Before Christ's crucifixion, He called out His assembly and instructed them to preach the gospel. But after Jesus was crucified and buried, no one was much interested in propagating their faith.

Had we been hunkering down with the early disciples in the days after Jesus' crucifixion, I doubt we would have foreseen much of a future for the church.

Dead leader. Running followers. End of story. Right?

Wrong.

From a secular sense, the apostles didn't have the makings for becoming leaders of a great movement. They fled in the face of fear, hid in the aftermath of disappointment, and doubted in the face of triumph.

But the strength of the church has never been human. Jesus told us, "I am the vine, ye are the branches: He that abideth in me, and I in him, the same bringeth forth much fruit: for without me ye can do nothing" (John 15:5). And Paul reminded us that "the weapons of our warfare are not carnal, but mighty through God…" (2 Corinthians 10:4). The early church was rooted, fruitful, and replenishing, not primarily because of her human leadership, but because of the truth she possessed and the Holy Spirit who dispensed and propagated it.

> ...upon this rock I will build my church; and the gates of hell shall not prevail against it.—MATTHEW 16:18

> But ye shall receive power, after that the Holy Ghost is come upon you: and ye shall be witnesses unto me both in Jerusalem, and in all Judaea, and in Samaria, and unto the uttermost part of the earth.—ACTS 1:8

And so from the earliest days of the local church we see that her strength is in truth, and her power is in the resurrected Christ and the Holy Spirit.

WITHOUT, IN SPITE OF, AND BECAUSE

Without gospel tracts, without a printing press, and without the Internet, churches of the first century managed to spread the gospel and plant churches all throughout the Roman empire. Paul's epistles reference the fact that these first-century churches actually fulfilled the Great Commission in their generation.[4]

They accomplished this in spite of fierce persecution and deep suffering. Acts 8 records the intense persecution of first-century churches instigated by Paul (Saul), and history further records the brutalities they endured. Christians in the early Roman empire faced starving lions in the arena, were sentenced to labor as slaves in the mines, were exiled from home and provision, or were tortured beyond what paper and ink descriptions can reveal.

---

4   Romans 1:8; Colossians 1:6, 23; 1 Thessalonians 1:8

Being a Christian in the first century was far from a comfortable existence. Being an evangelistic Christian was even more difficult. And planting churches in pagan cities? It was only by the grace of God.

But the greatest danger to first-century New Testament churches was not the sword. It was a deadlier threat than execution—the greatest danger was compromise.

Because the apostles understood where the true strength of the church rested and because they discerned where her true enemies hid, they passionately warned the churches against false doctrine.[5] They immediately and thoroughly discipled new converts.[6] And they labored diligently to correct the twisted Gnostic and legalistic teachings that crept into the early churches.[7]

Clearly, early churches valued the gospel and loved the New Testament church.

UNDERGROUND

If hunkering down in the upper room with the disciples didn't shake your faith in the future of the early church, let's tunnel through the catacombs with the early Christians.

Terrie and I had the opportunity to visit these catacombs some years ago. Crouching there inside the heart of the earth, it is not difficult to imagine the fear of early Christians in hiding. These miles of excavated tunnels, which Christians carved through the soft volcanic rock outside the ancient city of Rome, are a

---

5   Acts 20:28–31; Philippians 3:2; Colossians 2:8; 2 Peter 3:16–18
6   Acts 18:11; 1 Thessalonians 2:11–12; 2 Timothy 2:2
7   See, in particular, the epistles of Galatians and 1 John.

lasting reminder to the persecution Christians endured through the second, third, and fourth centuries after Christ. The intricate systems, spanning a 590-acre area with tunnels layered one on top of another, served as secret meeting places for worship and burying places for their martyrs.

In spite of harsh persecution, these Christians kept the faith. Lions might have been able to tear their limbs, but no executioner could rip from their souls their faith in Christ.

BRIGHT LIGHTS SIGNALING DARK DAYS

To Christians in 313 AD, Constantine's Edict of Milan, granting tolerance to all religions, must have seemed a beacon of hope, a ray of sunshine never before imagined. To have freedom to worship unmolested? What a privilege!

But to the unregenerate Constantine, his edict was apparently shrewd politics. The early churches had been so successful in reproducing that Constantine saw in them the infrastructure to unify his empire. Thus, he legalized the religion that was already spreading and harnessed its network for civil purposes.

Am I harsh to thus judge Constantine's motives? One might think so…if it weren't for the facts of history. Even after Constantine's supposed conversion (which consisted of seeing a vision of a burning cross), he continued to worship pagan deities and engage in superstitious rituals.[8] Furthermore, he followed

---

8   Thomas Armitage, *A History of the Baptists*, (Baptist Heritage Press, 2 Volumes, 1988), 204–205.

the tradition of earlier emperors and insisted that he himself be worshiped.[9]

What Constantine launched quickly turned into a full-blown ecclesiastical monster—the state church. And so, for hundreds of years, the state protected its civil religion while simultaneously persecuting personal religion. State churches, of course, rapidly deteriorated from whatever vestiges of truth they may have once held. The very concept of the state church is fundamentally opposed to Christ being the head of the church (Ephesians 5:23; Colossians 1:18), and it lends itself to facilitating political expediency rather than promoting true worship. In fact, whatever the religion—Christianity, Islam, or even Atheism (such as Communism)—persecution is the sure child of a marriage between the government and religion.

> With courageous humility that found its strength in God, they stood for truth.

And so, what at first appeared to be a ray of hope turned into a shadow of death. These were dark days for Christians who embraced the basic doctrines of the New Testament church. Over the ensuing centuries, these Christians were persecuted and slaughtered literally by the *millions*.

And yet, scattered throughout Europe, Asia, and Africa were committed Christians—so dedicated to the truths of Scripture that their testimonies make me blush in shame. With courageous

---

9   Philip Schaff and David Schley Schaff, *History of the Christian Church* (Charles Scribner's Sons, 1910), 14–15.

humility that found its strength in God, they stood for truth. Although at times throughout the centuries their doctrine would become skewed (often because of the lack of training available), nothing but their love for Jesus and dedication to truth could keep them shining for Christ during these dark days. Such were the Paulicians, Montanists, Novatianists, and Donatists in Armenia (modern-day Georgia, Armenia, and Azerbaijan), the Albigenses in France, the Waldenses in Italy, and numerous other groups. We owe much to the courage of these people whom most of us have never honestly studied![10]

AFTER THE DARK AGES

Without question, 1517 was an epoch point in history—both secular and Christian. When Martin Luther posted his Ninety-Five Theses, he challenged the corrupted doctrine of the state church. As the Reformation gained support and the reformers continued to protest the abuses of the Roman Catholic Church (often paying for their protests with their blood), the tight grasp of the state church began to weaken.

The Reformation truly did weaken the power of the Pope. Alongside that benefit came a trend toward the strengthening of freedom for true religion.

But there was a flip side to the Reformation—it wasn't all beneficial. The Reformation actually conceived more of what it

---

10 For a book-length overview on the history of the local, New Testament church, see *A Glorious Church* by Mike Gass, published by Striving Together Publications.

attempted to reform—state churches.[11] Yes, the reformers argued against and stood for some of the landmark doctrines of the Christian faith (especially, salvation through faith alone), but they had little or garbled understanding of what a true church looked like.

Before the Reformation, during the Reformation, and after the Reformation, there were churches that were functioning completely unidentified with and in doctrinal opposition to the Roman Catholic Church. To the government, Christians in these churches (as well as others who attempted to reform the government churches from within) were a threat. During and after the Reformation, these Christians were heavily persecuted by the various state churches across Europe.

I have visited Bunhill Fields, the famous burying place in London for nonconformists; stood in Bedford Prison, where John Bunyan penned *Pilgrim's Progress;* and viewed the Limmat River in Zurich where Felix Manz was drowned. For these "Baptist forefathers," the Great Reformation was not as exciting as it looks in the pages of a history book. For them, state churches meant imprisonment, being burned at the stake, and being drowned *by the reformers themselves.*[12] Zealous as the reformers were, they didn't understand New Testament church doctrine. By creating their own state churches, they perpetuated the persecution that follows the establishment of state religion.

---

11   Several leaders during the Reformation began their own state churches which ultimately led to the persecution of Anabaptists. John Knox began the Presbyterian church, Martin Luther the Lutheran church, King Henry VIII the Anglican church. These state churches essentially marked the beginning of denominations as we know them today.

12   *A Glorious Church,* 175, 181–182, 183.

The churches that by and large held New Testament doctrine concerning both salvation and the church called themselves by various names throughout the Reformation—Waldensians, Moravians, Mennonites, and several others. Enemies of these groups, gave them another name—*Anabaptist. Ana* meaning "twice" or "again," this title signified the Anabaptists were baptizing converts who had once been "baptized" as infants.

The "Anabaptists" themselves preferred the simple title "Baptists." After all, the infant baptism was not even scriptural baptism; thus, they were not *re*baptizing.[13] And so it was that the name *Baptist* was popularized through the very people who wished to end our doctrine.[14]

Even in the early American colonies, state churches flexed their muscles. The devout Puritans whipped, imprisoned, fined, and banished Baptists by the scores.[15]

One of the most notable and remembered Baptists in early American history is Roger Williams, founder of the Rhode Island colony who planted what many consider the earliest Baptist church in America. There were others, too, who stood for Baptist truth. With courage and faith, they slowly made progress as they established house churches, baptized converts, and planted new local churches. I'm thankful today for the persistent and obedient faith of these early American Baptists.

---

13   Thomas Armitage, *A History of the Baptists, Volume 1* (Bryan Taylor & Co., 1886), 327–328.

14   Anne Dunan-Page, *Grace Overwhelming: John Bunyan, "The Pilgrim's Progress" and the Extremes of the Baptist Mind* (Peter Lang, AG, International Academic Publishers, 2006), 95–96.

15   Francis J. Bremer, *Puritans and Puritanism in Europe and America: A Comprehensive Encyclopedia* (ABC-CLIO, 2006), 569. Also see *A History of the Baptists, Volume 2* by John T. Christian, (Broadman Publishing, 1926), especially chapters 1–3.

IF TRUTH IS WORTH BELIEVING...

Looking back over the centuries, from the upper room to the catacombs to the Inquisition prison chambers to the Reformation drownings to the First Amendment of the American constitution, the fact that New Testament churches have survived at all is amazing. But even more stunning is that they propagated themselves in the process.

Today, at least in America, we have the privilege of holding the torch of truth against a smoother landscape than our forefathers. Sometimes I fear that freedom itself becomes a mixed blessing because it tends to a decline in fervency. That which our forefathers suffered for, we simply enjoy. And the outcome is that we tend to get distracted from the core principles and truths of our faith.

> Millions have believed the authority of God's Word so strongly that they were willing to die for its truths.

I wonder sometimes, with all the church growth philosophies that bring more and more of the world into the church, and with the prevalence of watered-down preaching in our pulpits, how many Christians even know what we stand for? And I wonder how many of us would stand for the truth in the face of persecution if it came to that here in America?

In the midst of our culture's "let the good times roll" mentality, we need to treasure the truth and preach doctrine. The New Testament church position has been one of revering God's Word and elevating it above all else—including freedom, including tradition, including personalities.

The Waldensians who said, "Our tears…choke our very hearts" were not choked in heart over preaching styles, petty issues, or institutional affiliations. It was a commitment to Christ that led our forefathers to the stake, held them under the water to be drowned, and kept them strong in prison.

Arnold of Brescia,[16] William Tyndale,[17] Jan Block,[18] Felix Mantz,[19] Anne Askew,[20] and millions of others believed the authority of God's Word so strongly that they were willing to die for its truths. These men and women stood for the inspiration of Scripture, salvation through the blood of Christ apart from the sacraments, the biblical Lord's Table, and the priesthood of the believer. Their sacrifices stand as a stirring reminder to the importance of biblical Baptist distinctives.

Our heritage is a legacy of people who believed in truth. It is a heritage larger than personalities or preferences, but one that is absolutely committed to Scripture and to principle. As we now consider a brief history of the independent Baptist movement, remember the high price that was paid for the truth and the commitment of godly people to contend for the faith.

---

16 J. Newton Brown, *Memorials of Baptist Martyrs* (American Baptist Publication Society, 1854), 40–42.

17 William Tyndale, *The Obedience of a Christian Man* (originally published in 1528, Digireads.com, 2012), 69–70. Also Fran Rees, *William Tyndale: Bible Translator and Martyr* (Compass Point Books, 2006), 79–86

18 Thielem J. Von Bracht, translated by I. Daniel Rupp, *The Bloody Theatre* (David Miller, 1837), 810–812.

19 J. Newton Brown, *Memorials of Baptist Martyrs*, 49–54.

20 *Ibid.*, 270–280.

COOPERATION AND CONVENTIONS

While Baptists believe in local church autonomy, we have always been glad to work in loose cooperation with other Baptist churches for a cause. Historically, that cause has been evangelization, especially missions.

In fact, early Baptist churches in America formed the Triennial Convention in 1814 expressly for the purpose of sending missionaries. Its official name was "General Missionary Convention of the Baptist Denomination in the United States of America for Foreign Missions."[21]

The group got off to a good start, but in the ensuing decades, tensions rose between churches over the issue of slavery. When the Baptist churches of the North refused to support slave-holding missionaries through the moneys of the convention, the churches of the South broke from the convention. In 1845, they established the Southern Baptist Convention. (Incidentally, the northern convention changed its name in 1907 to the Northern Baptist Convention. Today it identifies itself as American Baptist Churches USA.)

On the technical side of facts, the convention in the North was looser, primarily an affiliation to support missions. The convention in the South was established with more control over the churches from the very beginning, something that Southern churches had wished for when they were part of the earlier convention. Churches on both sides maintained that they were still autonomous. But, as time would tell, it would be pretty tough to go against the wishes of the convention…or the doctrine.

---

21   William H. Brackney, *Historical Dictionary of the Baptists* (Scarecrow Press, 2009), 246.

A MODERN MONSTER

As the Civil War ended and the era of Reconstruction began, a formidable monster bullied his way into American churches. His name was Modernism, and he insisted on the ideals of German rationalism and higher criticism.

Modernism had been eroding European theology for years, but it wasn't until after our Civil War that it became a serious threat in American churches. Up to this point, our nation's Christian heritage was apparent in most venues of American society. Through the influence of the Puritans, the Great Awakening revivals, and the evangelistic efforts of Christians, the greater portion of Americans esteemed and reverenced Scripture—even if they were not "religious" or part of a church.

But in the 1870s, a nationwide drift from our early moorings became apparent. With the wide circulation of Charles Darwin's *The Origin of the Species* and a heavy cultural emphasis on the supremacy of science, Christians struggled to reconcile secularistic science and faith. Many began to promote allegorical interpretations of Scripture, thus hoping to alleviate the tension between what the Bible actually said and what current science suggested. This approach to Scripture spilled into every area of doctrine, including (and especially) creation and eschatology.

Leading pastors shifted their preaching from literal, practical, specific declarations of Scripture to idealistic, social, allegorical speeches. This disturbing phenomenon, triggering a landslide of liberalism, was not limited to one group or denomination. It infiltrated all denominations and even became a serious threat in the Baptist conventions.

It is important to understand that Modernism was an all-out affront against the clear and plain truths of Scripture. It did not represent slight differences of opinion on minor scriptural applications or practices—it had to do with the validity and authenticity of Scripture itself.

TO FIGHT THE MONSTER

As the monster of Modernism gained ground in denominations and churches across the country, wise Christians grew increasingly alarmed. With determination and a love for truth, they began forming affiliations to fight the liberal theology that was running rampant. They did not form a denomination, but a movement—a common stand for a common cause.

Seeing the situation for what it was—an aspect of spiritual warfare—these bold men saw their role as a fight for the faith, and they responded with a militancy for truth. In 1909, A. C. Dixon and R. A. Torrey began to compile and publish what would become a twelve-volume set titled *The Fundamentals: A Testimony to the Truth*. Lyman and Milton Stewart, brothers and Christian laymen, financed this project and paid for its free distribution.[22]

These articles featuring the work of many authors underscored five nonnegotiable tenets of the Christian faith. Collectively, they came to be known as the "Five Points of Fundamentalism."[23]

---

22 George M. Marsden, *Fundamentalism and American Culture* (Oxford University Press, 1980), 118–119.

23 Harriet A. Harris, *Fundamentalism and Evangelicals* (Oxford University Press, 1998), 25–26.

1. The inerrancy of Scripture
2. The virgin birth of Christ
3. The substitutional atonement of Christ
4. The bodily resurrection and future second coming of Christ
5. The authenticity of the biblical miracles

As you can see, the five truths chosen pertained specifically to the authenticity of Scripture and to salvation itself. These beliefs are necessary for one to be an orthodox Christian. Of course, a person may subscribe to all five of these truths intellectually and *not* be born again, but he cannot deny them and be saved. However, Baptists have always believed far more than this basic list. We would also include important doctrines pertaining to baptism by immersion, the autonomy of the New Testament church, etc. But in the early twentieth century, *anyone* who was against Modernism and who believed in the five truths mentioned above wanted to identify themselves as a "fundamentalist." This was not perceived as a full statement of faith, but as a stand against all that liberalism represented. By and large, the strongest fundamentalists were Presbyterians, Methodists, and Baptists.

Among the Baptists themselves, the clash between the liberals and the fundamentals waged strong. Especially in the North, prominent Baptist pastors who had wealthy donors supporting them preached liberal doctrine. These pastors included such men as Henry Ward Beecher and Harry Emerson Fosdick.

A tipping point for the Baptist churches who were affiliated with the Northern Baptist Convention was when Fosdick preached the sermon "Shall the Fundamentalists Win?" in 1922. Although many Northern Baptists—pastors and laymen—*were* fundamentalists, they did not constitute the financial backbone of the convention, and thus liberalism was the new norm.

Soon, liberalism pushed its way into the Southern Baptist Convention as well. As standing for truth within the convention became less and less plausible, pastors began to consider their options.

STRENGTH IN AUTONOMY

Godly pastors by the scores began to pull their churches out of the Northern Baptist Convention in the 1930s. By the 1940s, pastors within the Southern Baptist Convention also chose to leave the convention rather than compromise the faith once delivered unto the saints.[24]

The churches' grievances against the conventions included the following:

- They collected churches' missions moneys and used it to support missionaries who didn't believe the gospel or the fundamentals of the faith.
- They corrupted the young minds of students in their seminaries—young people who had been mentored and trained by fundamental pastors—teaching them straight, unadulterated liberalism.
- They elected men to leadership positions within the conventions who literally disbelieved the Bible and the gospel.

---

24   See *In Pursuit of Purity* by David O. Beale (Unusual Publications, 1986) for a more thorough treatment of fundamentalists who left liberal conventions.

As churches around the nation broke their ties to the conventions, in many cases, they formed loose fellowships for the cause of missions and education. The largest of these fellowships —the Baptist Bible Fellowship (BBF)—traces its origins to one of the most well-known Baptist pastors of the 1900s—J. Frank Norris.

The fellowship which Norris actually founded was the World Baptist Fellowship. Norris' bold preaching and unapologetic stand for fundamental doctrine and practice attracted hundreds of Baptist pastors who were experiencing unrest in their spirit over the doctrinal compromises within the Southern Baptist Convention. Through leaving the convention himself and through his preaching and leadership skills, Norris blazed the trail toward independence.

Over time, the World Baptist Fellowship struggled over mounting logistical and financial tensions. In a 1950 pastors' meeting, these tensions came to a head, and G. B. Vick (a previous president within this group) launched the BBF, which still exists today.

What were these non-convention Baptists to be called? It was pretty obvious: they were, of course, fundamental (this is why they left their conventions). And now, without identifying themselves by a convention, they were also independent. And above all, they were *Baptist.* Thus, they were "independent, fundamental Baptists." These were words that clearly identified them as Bible-believing men who belonged to unaffiliated churches.

STRENGTHS OF INDEPENDENT BAPTISTS

Those early independent fundamental Baptist pastors who left their conventions were men of great faith. Convention leaders told them they were committing "career suicide" when they left—and with good reason, too. They lost church buildings (many were actually owned by the convention), parsonages, retirement plans, and the security of being backed by the convention. Some were able to pull their churches out of the convention; some were voted out of their churches and had to plant new churches from scratch.

Independent fundamental Baptist churches in the early half of the last century were characterized by store-front churches, passionate pastors, fervent soulwinning zeal...and, in many cases, numerically growing churches. God blessed these people who honored Him by placing doctrine above position and seeking His approval more than the approval of a group. Independent fundamental Baptist churches grew quickly and notably.

As churches pulled out of the conventions, they found they once again promoted the strength of the local church and the headship of Christ. Two of the immediately apparent strengths of the independent movement among Baptists (which are still two of our greatest strengths today) were in missions and soulwinning.

In missions, independent Baptists follow the biblical model of a local church sending a missionary to plant churches worldwide. The missionary visits and receives support from other churches. This model allows churches to have regular interaction with missionaries, bringing Christians face-to-face with the largeness of the world and their responsibility to obey the Great Commission. It also challenges young people toward missions. The result is that independent Baptist churches tend to be missions-minded. In fact, per capita, I would venture to say that they lead the nation in missions giving and sending.[25]

Additionally, independent Baptist churches have had a sustained fervor for soulwinning for many years. More than any affiliation that I know of, independent Baptist churches have worked to centralize their focus on reaching people with the gospel. Many of them have scheduled times for outreach and are purposeful and aggressive in saturating their communities with the gospel. They reach out to the poor, neglected, and downtrodden of their communities through bus, addiction, prison, and nursing home ministries.

> Two of the greatest strengths among independent Baptists are missions and soulwinning.

And one more strength of independent Baptists is that they tend to be sensitive to doctrinal error. Because there is no denominational board to leave doctrinal decisions to, independent churches exercise great vigilance in guarding the faith—earnestly contending for the truths of Scripture (Jude 3).

HERITAGE AND FUTURE

When I look at the history of fundamentalism, independent churches, and Baptists, I'm more thankful than ever for my heritage

---

25 A statistic like this is admittedly difficult to verify as independent Baptists do not report either their sending or giving to a central location. Available information, however, as well as my experience with many independent Baptist fellowships across the nation seem to indicate this to be true.

and beliefs. The founding beliefs of our movement trace much further back than the 1870s or the 1930s. I believe they go all the way back to the New Testament.

- Fundamental—literal belief in the core doctrines of the Bible
- Independent—autonomous, self-governing New Testament churches
- Baptist—doctrine and practice that holds Scripture alone as the final authority

These have been and are the three key principles of biblical churches. Although known by different titles in different periods of history, these are the principles over which godly leaders have given their lives rather than sacrifice these truths. These are the principles over which early leaders of the independent fundamental Baptist movement decided they would prefer to commit career suicide than to compromise.

I believe in these principles. I believe they are biblical. I believe they are essential to authentic local church ministry.

Enjoy Biblical Fellowship

THE MOUNTAINTOP OF THE YEAR—literally and spiritually—for men in our church is our annual Men and Boys Campout. And this will be our twenty-seventh summer to head up to the Sierra Nevada Mountains for a weekend of preaching and growth.

Our campsite has no running water, no toilets, no anything—not even cell phone service. Just sky and trees and mountains and fishing. We bring tents, blankets, fishing poles, and food. And some of us have taken to bringing RVs—the really wimpy guys book a nearby motel. We have an unforgettable weekend of activity, preaching services, and campfires.

It's a joy to watch the men and boys of our church make memories together, climaxed by the thrill of watching hundreds of men, young and old alike, respond to the preaching of God's Word. Every year, I talk to scores of men who have come to a crossroads in their spiritual journeys. And every year, I have the privilege of opening God's Word and sharing His truth with men who know they need it. Over the course of those two days, in response to preaching and counseling, men make decisions that transform their lives, marriages, and homes and bear fruit for years to come.

Yes, the campout is good. In fact, uncomfortable as the campsite may be, each year it seems the weekend comes to a close all too soon.

But end it does. We pack our gear, load into our vehicles, and drive back down the mountain to live the decisions we've made.

Really, it would be counter-productive to stay on the mountain. The whole purpose of the campout is to encourage men to make decisions for off-mountain living.

FELLOWSHIP'S DANGEROUS COUSIN

Christian fellowship is one of the richest gifts of the Christian life. The early church knew and practiced it as "they continued steadfastly in the apostles' doctrine and fellowship, and in breaking of bread, and in prayers" (Acts 2:42). I treasure fellowship with my church family and with hundreds of pastors and Christian friends who love and serve God. I believe we as Christians and as spiritual leaders need the strength of authentic relationships.

But along the way among independent fundamental Baptists, the Christian fellowship enjoyed by likeminded pastors and churches has been blighted by a destructive phenomenon. The "fellowships" have often transformed into isolated "camps." The damage is predictable.

Just as a weekend camping trip loses its purpose when it becomes a lifestyle of tent-dwelling, so Christian fellowship becomes damaging when it morphs into long-term identity rather than encouraging support. In other words, I'm all for "camping" and "fellowshipping;" but I'm not all about becoming a squatter or part of a particular "camp." In so doing, we forfeit our ability to move forward as autonomous churches for Christ. We tie ourselves by becoming more engaged with how our "camp" is doing than by encouraging good, likeminded leaders who are also sound, doctrinal Baptists.

HOW FELLOWSHIPS BECOME CAMPS

Independent Baptists in the earlier half of the twentieth century were characterized by commitment to principle. Men who left the conventions walked away from large churches, security, and bright futures to start all over again in storefronts and poverty. God blessed these humble beginnings with marked growth.

Before long, the storefronts transformed again into large churches—in many cases, larger than the churches the pastors had left. Young preachers were eager to join a growing movement that was scripturally solid and growth oriented.

And then, the tragic inevitable (considering human nature) happened. Over the past few decades, camps began to develop as strong personalities received loyalty from younger preachers. Soon, distinct camps began to develop.

Although camps don't have the paperwork ties of conventions, their invisible ties tend to put an "independent" church into a box. This time, the groupings weren't around a convention, but around personalities, colleges, or issues. These unhealthy groupings developed their own definition of *fundamentalism*, and being labeled as "liberal" wasn't so much about doctrine anymore as it was about strong preferences, personal beliefs, personality, or institution alliances. The term *liberal* came to mean "someone who doesn't support our group."

Unfortunately, some preachers in particular groups believed that the functional practices of their group *was* fundamentalism. ("If you have the same standards as me, you must be a fundamentalist as well; if not, you're probably a liberal—or at least suspect.") In some groups, standards of dress became the networking issue. Other groups have been formed around the feeling "old fashioned," dictatorial leadership styles, or resistance to technology. Some groups have been formed around types of ministry practices (i.e. the emphasis in your church on the bus ministry or if your church uses an organ). Many of these issues have been extrabiblical; some have been downright ridiculous.

> Man-centered loyalty tends to divide personalities rather than establish truth.

Some of the grouping would be understandable—if it were only an issue of fellowship. For instance, my closest friends in the ministry are obviously going to be those with whom I have the most in common. God has used various independent Baptist fellowships in a great way over the years. To the extent that these fellowships bring servant-hearted leaders together for the furtherance of the gospel, that's biblical and helpful. But once grouping becomes an issue of loyalty, an unhealthy camp is established. Of course, loyalty to camps defuses proper loyalty to Jesus as the true head of the local church.[1]

LEADERSHIP AND RELATIONSHIPS

Two of the subtle losses to our movement through the camp mentality are servant leadership and authentic ministry relationships.

A leader who hopes for a following must maintain a "mystique." He feels the need to remain aloof, and he is conscious of his image and the image of his ministry. The by-product of this pride is that he cuts himself off from the needful relationships leaders need for accountability, personal encouragement, and growth.

Boastful, fleshly approaches to leadership create an environment of competition, division, and dissension. Strange as it may seem, the very nature of "camps" has cut us off from true fellowship, and it has tended to devalue authentic relationships. When image building substitutes for fellowship, a significant personal anchor is lost, giving the devil entrance into one's heart and ministry.

WHAT THE BIBLE SAYS ABOUT CAMPS

Man-centered loyalty tends to divide personalities rather than establish truth. At least that's what it did in Corinth. Both the Apostle Paul and his helper Apollos had labored in the Corinthian

---

1   Colossians 1:18

church. They had both served with gospel-centered ministry philosophies. And they both praised God for the increase.

But for the Corinthian church, it wasn't enough that both men had the same goal in mind. Christians in this church picked up on subtle differences between those who cared for their spiritual health. Whatever the differences were, they were minor enough that Paul counted Apollos a co-laborer; yet they were significant enough that someone was able to create a distinction obvious enough for church members to take sides. And take sides they did. When the issue of discussion would surface, one member would say, "I am of Paul." "Who cares?" a member of the opposing opinion would retort. "I'm of Apollos, and he is just as good a Christian as Paul." A few claimed Peter (Cephas) as their "camp leader," and the ones who considered themselves *really* spiritual would counter, "I follow *Christ*."[2]

And what was Paul's response? "For ye are yet carnal: for whereas there is among you envying, and strife, and divisions, are ye not carnal, and walk as men? For while one saith, I am of Paul; and another, I am of Apollos; are ye not carnal? Who then is Paul, and who is Apollos, but ministers by whom ye believed, even as the Lord gave to every man" (1 Corinthians 3:3–5).

Paul was unimpressed with camps. Actually, he was *anti*-camps.

Camps don't look so bad at the onset. They form over issues that are distinct enough that those on the inside have strong reasons for being there, and those on the outside (or in an opposing camp) have strong reasons for remaining where they are.

Churches within camps are in danger of losing their autonomy. They are prone to remain dependent on the opinions and direction

---

2   1 Corinthians 1:12

of the camp. And most grievously, they create unnecessary divisions, foster jealousy, and feed pride. They might hold to sound doctrine, but all too often they model James' description of fleshly wisdom: "But if ye have bitter envying and strife in your hearts, glory not, and lie not against the truth. This wisdom descendeth not from above, but is earthly, sensual, devilish. For where envying and strife is, there is confusion and every evil work" (James 3:14–16).

I understand that people use the word *camps* in different contexts. Some use it in reference to biblical fellowship or to denote similar ministry philosophy. For instance, there are circles within our movement with whom I have closer fellowship; and there are people who claim a similar title with whom I don't want to be associated. I'm not wanting to make the words *camp* and *fellowship* a matter of tight semantics. I'm

> Churches within camps are in danger of losing their autonomy.

merely pointing out that petty envy and strife over personalities, institutions, or minor issues is not of God. Furthermore, it has created unhealthy and extraordinarily damaging effects within our movement. The issue here is not with whom you fellowship. It is why and if you have to label everyone else who is *not* in your "camp."

For much of my ministry, I have striven to enjoy Christian fellowship while avoiding the camp mentality. Not in the "ultra-spiritual" claims of Corinth, but I want to identify with *Jesus…* outside the camp. "Wherefore Jesus also, that he might sanctify the people with his own blood, suffered without the gate. Let us go forth therefore unto him without the camp, bearing his reproach"

(Hebrews 13:12–13). I thank God for the gift of fellowship and for the many gracious influences He has allowed on my life and ministry. But I want to have the freedom to follow Him without the fear of man that goes with the camp mentality.

BRANDED IDENTITY

Thanks to camps and loud allegiances over non-doctrinal issues, our movement has developed a branded reputation. Through pride, unnecessary divisions, jealousy, moral failures, and ministry philosophies that had little emphasis on discipleship and sound preaching, we have lost influence while gaining a reputation.

In the last few decades, words that began as terms to describe our core principles—independent fundamental Baptist—have over time morphed into a moniker for a perceived network or affiliation.

To many outsiders "independent fundamental Baptist" actually *is* a denomination—or at the least an organized convention.

To those within "camps," their circle within independent fundamental Baptist churches is indeed an unofficial network. They ascribe loyalty to camp leaders and make decisions based less on Scripture and more on the general practice of the group.

To those of us who still see "independent fundamental Baptist" as a simple description of what we believe and how we practice, the perceived affiliations are disturbing.

The very reason I am an independent Baptist is because it has never been my belief or intention to be part of any such group identity. The words that were formerly descriptive terms have now become a brand. And, frankly, I don't want to be branded with or by other churches, camps, individuals, or networks. I want to be identified by what I believe—not by a perceived network. I believe in autonomy—not brands.

CAMPS AND CAMPOUTS

Later in this book we will examine specific imbalances that have damaged our movement. We'll look at our dangerous, fleshly tendencies and their disastrous outcomes.

But before you turn the page, I'd like to invite you to look at this next section as a "personal campout"—a retreat in which you open your heart for the Holy Spirit's inspection. It's easy for all of us to point out the error of others (especially those who are in another "camp"), but it's more humbling to admit that perhaps we have made a wrong turn or two ourselves. In fact, we might have even veered way off course. If we are ever to discard the damaging and divisive camp mentality, it will only be because we faithfully take brief campouts to allow God to search and cleanse our hearts and then lead us forward for Him.

Confront False Teaching and Sin

A s a sophomore in Bible college, I received a call from the dean of students. He wanted me to meet him in his office as soon as possible. Not the kind of call most college sophomores get excited about.

But contrary to my expectations, that meeting turned out to be a turning point in my college life.

"There is a group of several elderly ladies down by Coachella, California (about 150 miles from our college), who are asking us to send a preacher to hold services. Would you be interested in leading a group of students down this weekend?"

Would I?! This opportunity was nothing short of a thrill for me. Long story short, over the next several months, the tiny group of ladies grew into several dozen people, and I was pastoring my first church.

Before long, we were outgrowing the living room where we met and were ready to move into something larger. We purchased a doublewide trailer, hauled it to property that had been donated to the church, and scheduled a men's workday to ready our new building for use.

I arrived for the workday only to discover that I was the only worker! Working solo in the 115 degree heat, I began the arduous task of positioning railroad ties underneath the trailer.

An hour or so into my labor, who should show up to help but Howard. Howard was a nice guy, and I was glad he was part of our church. He struggled, however, with mental challenges and was extremely uncoordinated. I appreciated his spirit, but I wished for more help!

> False teachers do not advertise themselves as such.

I briefed Howard on the process of moving the beams under the trailer, and he responded with enthusiasm. I directed him around the trailer to the other side of the beam that I had been working into place. With a "one-two-three, heave!" I forced all my strength against the beam. It barely budged.

"One-two-three, heave!" I called again, and I dug my heels deeper into the hot sand and pushed harder.

Strange, we don't seem to be making any progress. And then a discouraging suspicion formed in my mind. On our next heave, I peered under the trailer at Howard. Sure enough, he was pushing the opposite direction that I was pushing.

Howard grinned as he saw me. "Isn't this fun, Pastor?"

Um, *fun* wasn't quite the word that came to my mind.

If there was ever a day that I wanted a worker to just quit, it was then.

Quit is not a word I like to use, and it's rarely an option that I suggest. In fact, as it relates to preachers, I've invested much of my life encouraging preachers *not* to quit. Through fellowship and friendship, books, conferences, and especially our Bible college, I've attempted to encourage preachers to be faithful in their service to the Lord—even during times of discouragement.

But, like Howard's help on the trailer, there are some preachers whose efforts are so counterproductive to our cause that I wish they would just throw in the towel!

One of the biggest challenges we face in witnessing today is the proliferation of church leaders who have lived immoral or otherwise biblically inconsistent lives. These leaders do great damage to the name of Christ. Their mishandling of God's Word and their ungodly lifestyles and attitudes distract the lost from the gospel.

Frankly, I wish every one of them would quit.

THINGS ARE NOT ALWAYS AS THEY APPEAR

Of course, false teachers do not advertise themselves as such. They don't add a "top 500 false teacher" badge to their websites or include "religious seducer" in their social networking bios. They might use picketing as one of their strategies, but they definitely don't wear a sandwich sign advertising "I am a gospel phony."

The presence of teachers who preach false doctrine or espouse biblically inconsistent philosophies is why we must learn to practice discernment. Paul explained to the church at Philippi what he was praying for them: "that your love may abound yet more and more in knowledge and in all judgment; That ye may approve things that are excellent; that ye may be sincere and without offence till the day of Christ" (Philippians 1:9–10). Paul wanted these Christians to abound in love, but he emphasized that theirs should be a *discerning* love.

More than ever before, Christians, especially Baptists, and especially independent Baptists, must clearly articulate our position and guard our spirit. We must "be ready always to give an answer to every man that asketh you a reason of the hope that is in you with meekness and fear" (1 Peter 3:15). And we must be ready to give that answer with a right spirit.

Our church members deserve to know where we stand on issues that unbiblical teachers have clouded. They need to understand that just because we have the same label as a false teacher does not mean that we believe the same thing.

So who is it that I wish would quit?

PREACHERS WHO SENSATIONALIZE

Jude 16 speaks of these men who are "murmurers, complainers, walking after their own lusts; and their mouth speaketh great swelling words, having men's persons in admiration because of advantage." These men use their positions in the ministry to sensationalize and exaggerate things to build themselves up. They have a personal agenda—stemming from and fueled by their ego.

Preachers who sensationalize issues to gain a following or to gain publicity are generally self-promoting narcissists. They endeavor to gain attention rather than to be faithful to the Word of

God. They use "great swelling words of vanity" to impress ignorant people (2 Peter 2:18). While their words or the issues on which they pin them may be impressive, they fail to preach the gospel itself.

For instance, think of Westboro Baptist Church in Topeka, Kansas, and what comes to mind? Your first thought probably turns to their maddening and dishonoring practice of picketing the funerals of our fallen heroes in the most offensive of methods and with belligerent attitudes. But an article which I recently read included another tidbit of information as an immediate association with this group.

> Westboro Baptist Church, the tiny independent fundamentalist Christian church based in Topeka, Kan., announced on Twitter that, once again, they are planning to stomp over our nation's heartache by protesting at the funerals of the victims of the Sandy Hook Elementary School shooting and declaring "God sent the shooter."—**The Washington Post**[1]

Did you catch that? The author of this article immediately identified Westboro Baptist Church as "independent fundamentalist...." But certainly we don't *want* to be associated with the hateful (even illogical) actions of this group in any way whatsoever! Honestly, a statement like the one in the article above gives me pause before using the word *fundamental* in describing myself to any unsaved person who may have just read this article.

---

1   Elizabeth Tenety, "Westboro Baptist Church to picket Sandy Hook funerals: 4 ways to respond," The Washington Post, December 17, 2012, http://www. washingtonpost.com/blogs/under-god/post/westboro-baptist-church-to-picket-sandy-hook-funerals-4-ways-to-respond/2012/12/17/520a6ba0-488e-11e2-b6f0-e851e741d196_blog.html.

Another author recently suggested, "You see, whether the anti-gay movement and the biblical literalists of our country like it or not, Westboro Baptist Church has become their most visible and vocal mouthpiece."[2]

I'm with the Apostle Peter—I wish the preachers who speak "great swelling words of vanity" would quit. Preachers who sensationalize—making one or two non-gospel issues the defining and divisional point of their ministries—frustrate the efforts of the rest of us.

Fred Phelps, pastor of Westboro Baptist Church, isn't the only pastor who is a sensationalist. He just happens to be out there, his high visibility making him one of the easiest to recognize and name. Anyone who marginalizes the message of the gospel by making the message more about a particular sin, current issue, or political stance is doing more to hurt the cause than to help it.

Please understand. I'm not one bit against Americans exercising their freedom of speech to picket for just çauses, and I'm definitely not against publicly standing for the truth of the gospel. But I am against doing so in a hateful way that dishonors and misrepresents Christ. Picketing a military funeral does nothing to help the public understand Christ's love, their sin, or salvation through Jesus' blood. It simply makes Christianity repulsive to the world.

I preach against sin. From Scripture, I address specific sinful lifestyles. I speak up about how Scripture applies to current issues and to political unrest that involves Christianity or Israel. And yet,

---

2   Paul Brandeis Raushenbush, "Thank You Westboro Baptist Church!" Huffington Post, January 2, 2013, http://www.huffingtonpost.com/paul-raushenbush/thank-you-westboro-baptist-church_b_2396991.html.

Lancaster Baptist Church is known as a church that cares for people and that actively, persistently shares the gospel. Yes, we must be the salt of the earth (Matthew 5:13), but we also must speak the truth in love (Ephesians 4:15).

Sensational preachers, however, are not the only group who I wish would quit.

PREACHERS WHO APOSTASIZE

These preachers are often men who at one time identified themselves as fundamentalists, but were either never saved or became full of bitterness and are now turned from the truth. They teach "damnable heresies, even denying the Lord that bought them" (2 Peter 2:1). They may have "a form of godliness" (2 Timothy 3:5), but they deny the power of the cross as they reject the core doctrines of the Christian faith, including the deity of Christ, the inspiration of Scripture, and salvation by grace through faith.

False teachers and apostates use people to their own personal gain. Second Peter 2:3 says of them: "through covetousness shall they with feigned words make merchandise of you." Charles Spurgeon wisely observed, "It is a remarkable fact that all the heresies which have arisen in the Christian church have had a decided tendency to dishonour God and to flatter man."[3]

I would add, too, that beyond learning to discern *people* who are apostates, we need to learn to discern their methods and philosophies. I'm deeply concerned when I see young preachers

---

3   Charles Spurgeon, *Spurgeon's Sermons Volume 6: 1860* (Christian Classics Ethereal Library), 666.

eagerly following after any new fad or method from popular evangelical leaders just because one of their churches appears successful. In some cases, the bestselling authors and prominent leaders espouse the very false doctrines and philosophy which Paul warned against. It is true that men who once claimed a belief in fundamental doctrine have and do slide to apostasy.

For instance, Norman Vincent Peale—a man who promoted positive thinking and limitless possibilities—rejected the doctrine of salvation by grace alone. On the Phil Donahue Show in 1984, Peale said, "It's not necessary to be born again. You have your way to God; I have mine. I found eternal peace in a Shinto shrine…I've been to Shinto shrines, and God is everywhere…."[4]

John Spong, an Episcopalian from New Jersey, has consistently written books that deny the virgin birth, the miracles, the Resurrection, and the Second Coming. Furthermore, he has stated that Paul and Timothy were homosexual lovers.[5]

There is no telling where apostasy will lead. From whatever circle of preachers or fellowship you find yourself receiving heavy input, I would encourage you to "try the spirits whether they are of God" (1 John 4:1). Even some mainline denominations have reprimanded some of the Reformed theologians in their midst who are leaning toward the dangers and heresies of the emergent church. Currently, I am observing a few Christian leaders as they endorse the false doctrine of the Roman Catholic Church. I sense that a spirit of apostasy will be prevalent in the days ahead.

---

4   Christian News, May 12, 1997, 11. Also see, Dave Hunt, "Revival or Apostasy," The Berean Call, October 1997, 2.

5   Tim LaHaye, *The Popular Handbook on the Rapture* (Harvest House Publishers, May 1, 2012), 181.

PREACHERS WHO RATIONALIZE

Rationalizing must be one of the most insidious sins of preachers—especially because a man who rationalizes preaches the truth with his mouth but denies it through his actions. Tragically, preachers who rationalize misrepresent God and corrupt the purity of the church.

I wish I could say this practice is rare. Although it has taken place in the minority of independent Baptist churches that I know of, it has prevailed in far too many churches and circles. Because it hits so close to home, I'm going to break the rationalizers into two categories:

Rationalizing immoral behavior

In some cases, pastors will rationalize allowing open, flagrant sin in the church to continue without confrontation, to please those who have influence—political or financial. Paul dealt with this issue in 1 Corinthians 5. The church at Corinth was aware of fornication taking place within the congregation, but the leadership would do nothing about it.

I have noticed an ironic tendency over years of ministry. Often, Christian leaders who emphasize and argue most vehemently over preference issues do so because they are covering real sin problems—their own sin or the sin of others close to them. I have known men who made a minor standard their weekly soapbox... only to be humiliated years later when their concurrent years of immoral failure were revealed.

As Matthew Henry observed, "The way to preserve the peace of the church, is to preserve the purity of it."[6] The presence of open or known sin that is ignored can quench the work of the Holy Spirit. We need His power in our churches more than we need anything or anyone! We dare not quench the very power that determines our success![7]

> "The way to preserve the peace of the church, is to preserve the purity of it."
>
> —Matthew Henry

I understand that dealing with sin issues is touchy and highly uncomfortable. But I'm not willing to waste my life attempting to lead God's people in my own strength. I'd rather seek His filling and wisdom to confront and counsel those who need help. Preachers who rationalize open sin in their church—preferring rather to turn the other way than to suffer loss by confrontation—stand by while the purity of the church is tarnished. Sooner or later (and often sooner than we realize), people begin to question the integrity of the pastor himself.

In my opinion, rationalizing known sin is one of the sad blights on Christianity today.

Rationalizing abuse

Another form of rationalization takes place when pastors are aware of an abusive and illegal situation but do not report it to authorities.

---

6   Matthew Henry, *An Exposition of All the Books of the Old and New Testaments* (Printed by and for W. Gracie, 1808), 54.

7   1 Thessalonians 5:19

This sin is often committed against children or minors—those vulnerable ones who most need our protection. Every young person deserves a loving and protective environment at home and at church (Matthew 19:13–14).

When it comes to sexual abuse, pastors simply must never rationalize saying, "Well, this is a family matter." Nor should they ever look the other way when a church worker violates the innocence of a young person. (See Matthew 18:6.) Spiritual leaders must stand in the gap to protect the young, vulnerable members of their flocks—even to the point of involving the authorities when it is legally required and/or would be helpful to the situation (Romans 13:3–4).

Media reporters who have caught wind of abuse that takes place under the spiritual oversight of Baptist churches have broad brushed all independent Baptists with the same stroke. I resent that. But at the same time, I grieve that the abuse has ever occurred.

I remember one news report in particular that highlighted several cases of abuse, including some allegedly occurring in independent fundamental Baptist churches. I felt there was improper and unfair reporting involved in the show. But the saddest outcome of it to me was not the biased reporting; it was the response of some independent Baptists. In the days following the show's release, pulpits were "hot" with preachers blasting the media. I know that part of their response was a knee-jerk reaction to the sting of injustice (being "lumped in" with abusers even though they were in no way affiliated). But I'm afraid we sent a very wrong message to our communities. If even a *fraction* of what was covered in the show was true, there was cause for deep, profound mourning. We should have expressed grief—not belligerence.

Every ministry should have a written policy in place to immediately report instances of sexual abuse and other criminal activity to local authorities. (See Appendix 5.) In many states, it is mandatory that those in the ministry report suspected child abuse or neglect. We are to be subject to the government God has ordained, for they are a "terror...to the evil" (Romans 13:3). This is vital for protecting children whom God has entrusted to our churches and for protecting the testimony of the church.

> Every ministry should have a written policy in place to immediately report instances of abuse.

Preachers who rationalize church sin or abuse grieve the Holy Spirit and severely limit their ministries and the power of Christ in their communities. Honestly, I wish they would quit preaching.

These three types of preachers—those who sensationalize, apostatize, and rationalize—hurt the name of Christ and confuse the lost.[8] Men, women, and sometimes children confronted with the inconsistencies and pride in these messages and lifestyles resolve that they don't want Christianity, and they reject Christ Himself.

PREACHERS WHO SHOULD CONTINUE

We must "be ready always to give an answer to every man that asketh you a reason of the hope that is in you with meekness and fear"

---

8   For a more thorough treatment of this concern, see blog post "How I Feel after a Pastor Falls," April 5, 2012, http://www.paulchappell.com/2012/08/05/how-i-feel-after-a-pastor-falls/.

(1 Peter 3:15). And in the midst of sensationalism, rationalization, and apostasy, sometimes that ready answer includes explaining to lost co-workers or family members why we do not identify with these false types of ministry and biblically defining our position by the true gospel.

I'm assuming that if you've read this far, you're *not* a preacher such as the ones described in this chapter. But in the next chapter, I'd like to challenge you in two ways: First, I challenge you to continue—to preach the Word. In this day of compromise, we need men with grace and courage to take the right stand in the right way, holding high the banner of the cross. Second, I challenge you to ask the Holy Spirit to reveal any imbalances in your heart or ministry He may wish to correct. Perhaps you would pause with me for a moment before beginning the next chapter and pray Psalm 139:23–24:

> Search me, O God, and know my heart: try me, and know
> my thoughts: And see if there be any wicked way in me,
> and lead me in the way everlasting.

Correct Imbalance in Ministry

HAVE YOU EVER CONSIDERED YOURSELF a funambulist? You are, you know. The day you became a Christian leader, you acquired the role of *funambulist* (not to be confused with *fundamentalist*)—a tight-rope acrobat. Derived from Latin roots, *funambulist* is comprised of the words *funis* (rope) and *ambulare* (walk). As spiritual leaders, it is our responsibility to walk with balance. Ephesians 5:15 puts it succinctly—"walk circumspectly."

Unfortunately, many independent fundamental Baptist leaders and ministries have lost their balance. In fact, I'd say that most of the eroding issues in our movement have been issues of balance. Along the way, we have shifted our focus from principles to preferences, from fellowship to camps, and from preaching and evangelism to creating a culture formed around topics. Rather than focusing on Jesus, preaching the gospel, and contending for the faith, we've become issue-oriented.

In this chapter, we will identify ten marks of imbalance in ministry. But first, let's identify what ideal ministry balance looks like.

DEFINING BALANCE

The target in every area of ministry is to be like Jesus. In fact, Jesus exemplified perfect balance. John 1:14 tells us He was "full of grace and truth."

We likewise need both grace and truth. More grace than truth, and we lean toward antinomianism. More truth than grace and we sway toward a legalistic philosophy.[1] The only solution is to be full of *both*. Only Christ exemplified this perfect balance, but we should be constantly growing in both grace *and* truth as we grow in His likeness. Paul indicated his desire to grow in his understanding of truth in Philippians 3:10–14. And we all claim the promise of James 4:6, "He giveth more grace."

---

1   Strictly defined, legalism is adding works to salvation. Legalism in this sense is firmly rebutted in the book of Galatians and all throughout the New Testament. There is, however, a sense in which we can become legalistic in our spirit by focusing on performance rather than elevating God's grace. This also is seen throughout the New Testament. For example, Jesus warned about the "tradition of the elders"—man-made rules that in some instances actually contradicted the law of God, and in other instances added to God's law (Matthew 15:1–8). Jesus also rebuked the Pharisees for adding extra-biblical rules that became burdensome and unhealthy (Matthew 23:4). As Bible-believing Baptists, we shun doctrinal legalism, but we don't always recognize what could be called "practical legalism."

A spirit of grace is humble, merciful, and generous. A commitment to truth means we stand firm on the Word of God and that we are committed to personal integrity.

The question is: how can we pursue both simultaneously? Additionally, how can we avoid the imbalances that are so sadly prevalent in churches today? For that matter, what *are* the core imbalances of ministering without grace and truth? And what are the signs that indicate we're slipping?

TAKE IT PERSONALLY

The ten points of imbalance I'm about to list could describe any one of several preachers or ministries that have collapsed and slipped off the tightrope. They may even remind you of existing ministries that you are sure are currently slipping. I assure you, however, that these chapters are not about any one person or ministry. They are about *me*. They are about *you*. They are about every Christian leader who has ever attempted to minister to God's people.

As you read, please don't make the mistake of dissecting others instead of inspecting yourself. Instead, obey the admonition of 1 Corinthians 10:12: "Wherefore let him that thinketh he standeth take heed lest he fall."

Some of my friends who have reviewed this book have suggested that most of these imbalances can be traced back to a few prominent leaders or ministries in fundamentalism. That may be true; nevertheless, we should examine our hearts closely for we are all susceptible to these sins of pride. The first tremors of imbalance on the wire are usually launched by the hideous, but too often unnoticed, sin of pride. Pride is the catapult for much of the unbalanced ministry that leads to compromised integrity. Pride precludes us from being filled with the grace we so desperately need to minister as Jesus would.

When our response to the Holy Spirit's faithful conviction is pride, we cut ourselves off from the One who gave us the privilege of serving as leaders. "God resisteth the proud, but giveth grace unto the humble" (James 4:6).

Over the years, when pride, rather than gratitude or a desire to deflect praise to God, has crept into my life, the Lord has graciously and faithfully convicted me. Because of all the Lord has needed to do in my life, I have endeavored to avoid fellowship with ministries where proud imbalances are the norm. Proverbs 22:24 also cautions against close associations with men who are consistently angry: "Make no friendship with an angry man; and with a furious man thou shalt not go."

I have asked the Holy Spirit, as well as godly friends and mentors, to point out prevalent proud imbalances in ministry— imbalances that reflect the opposite of humility before the Lord. In the spirit of a fellow funambulist who is still striving for balance and in need of God's grace, I share these ten marks of imbalance with you.[2]

Imbalance #1: Anger

I know, just designating this emotion as an imbalance has already aroused your righteous indignation! If truth were told, some independent Baptists view anger as something like the core of

---

2   For a condensed listing of these ten imbalances, see Appendix 2.

"real" preaching. I love strong biblical preaching where the Bible is supreme and doctrine is treasured—but neither of these is a call to personal offense. Far too often, anger in the pulpit is not over sin against God, but rather, it is a reaction to a perceived slight against ourselves, or even embarrassment. I'm afraid that anger has actually become an accepted norm in some fundamental churches. It's sort of the permissible sin.

It would be impossible to find scriptural support for the unspoken philosophy of leaders who seem to believe that being known as the meanest (especially in, although not necessarily limited to, the pulpit) is a badge of honor! The Bible, in fact, speaks contrariwise: " For the wrath of man worketh not the righteousness of God" (James 1:20). Churches with excessive anger can become abusive or manipulative. It is never the anger from the pulpit that produces godly conviction, repentance, and cleansing.

> Pride is the catapult for much of the unbalanced ministry that leads to compromised integrity.

One younger pastor recently commented to me about the toxicity of ministry cultures where the angry spirit drives prideful arrogance and judgment to the point that it becomes cannibalistic towards any and all differing views—even when those views are shared by leaders who have the same heart for God and the same beliefs in all doctrine and almost all areas of practice.

When a Christian (or an entire church or "fellowship") is known more for what he is *against* than what he is *for*, a definite and troubling imbalance is evidenced. What devastation for the world to associate a particular type of church with angry pulpits. Angry preaching (which is worlds apart from *passionate* preaching) is often, if not usually, a sign of an insecure pastor who attempts to motivate through guilt and shame rather than relying on the powerful grace of God.

While we share God's righteous anger against sin, we must avoid a persistently angry spirit. In some heartbreaking stories, leaders have even angrily separated from their own children or family members over differences in belief or practice. Being fundamental in doctrine has nothing to do with being angry in spirit; it has everything to do with believing what the Bible teaches.

Anger is one of the most destructive emotions of the flesh. Not only does it lead to bitterness, but it is sometimes a sign of deeper engagement with unconfessed moral sin. Both Hebrews 12 and James 3 identify this connection:

> Looking diligently lest any man fail of the grace of God; lest any *root of bitterness* springing up trouble you, and thereby many be defiled; Lest there be any *fornicator*…
> —HEBREWS 12:15–16

> But if ye have *bitter envying and strife in your hearts,* glory not, and lie not against the truth. This wisdom descendeth not from above, but is *earthly, sensual, devilish.* For where envying and strife is, there is confusion and *every evil work.*—JAMES 3:14–16

While I don't fully understand the link between the two, I have observed it repeatedly over the years. Fiercely angry men are often individuals who are stubbornly clinging to hidden sin. I see this in marriage counseling, and I witness it in counseling church leaders. I recently spoke with two assistant pastors whose senior pastor had resigned because of hidden moral sin in his life. The men shared that during staff meetings the senior pastor had often resorted to cursing at the staff in his anger.

Nobody had known just what to do in relation to those outbursts, but the pastor's anger and the ungodly expressions of it should have been a large red flag to the needs of his soul.

> When we become known for our anger, there is definite imbalance in our lives and ministries.

I'm not asserting that every preacher who evokes response through anger is involved in moral sin. But I am pointing out that when we become *known* for our anger, there is a definite imbalance in our lives and ministries. Perhaps this is why the qualifications for a pastor include that he be "no striker...patient, not a brawler" (1 Timothy 3:3). Of course, these are in the same checklist as the qualification "husband of one wife." Neither requirement is more important than the other—and together they produce balance. An angry spirit undermines our ability to lead with grace.

Imbalance #2: Concern for image over integrity

Man-centered ministries are driven by pride. Thus, the leaders of these ministries will do just about anything to protect their images.

Pride	Humility
Pride seeks to preserve an image of grace when in reality there is dark sin hiding.	Humility acknowledges the sin and seeks God's grace in dealing with that sin and in ministering to those hurt by it.
Pride works to convince others—both those within and those without the particular ministry— that the Christian leader or ministry is elite and perhaps even above reproach.	Humility acknowledges that we are nothing apart from God's grace and that without His ongoing work of sanctification in our hearts, we're in no shape to be used by Him.
Pride seduces us to believe lies about ourselves— that God is privileged to have us, that others should respect us for our spirituality, that we can continue in personal sin without consequences.	Humility positions us to humble ourselves, seek God's grace, and serve others in the fullness of the Spirit.

I recently read a book in which the author used an illustration to which I think all of us in ministry can relate.[3] He pointed out that when we first enter the ministry, we are consumed with the

---

3   Lance Witt, *Replenish: Leading from a Healthy Soul* (Baker Books, 2011), 32.

desire to preach Christ and make Him known. We know that Jesus is the true gift of the ministry, and we are eager and zealous to give others this incredible gift. But along the way, we tend to become more consumed with how the gift is packaged than the gift itself. We wrap the gift in packaging called "platform" or "programs" or "ministry philosophy"—none of which are wrong—but we must remember that they are only the packaging. The danger to which we too often succumb is our own tendency to focus more on keeping the wrapping looking good than to simply know Christ and to purely make Him known.

Grace-filled Christian leaders don't always have a shiny image and a large platform, but they do have the power of God working through them. In 2 Corinthians 9:8 we have the promise, "And God is able to make all grace abound toward you; that ye, always having all sufficiency in all things, may abound to every good work." It is this enabling grace which spiritual Christian leaders desire more than anything.

The Apostle Paul is an example of a spiritual leader whose personal integrity was impeccable. Even after years of ministry, Paul could say to Timothy, who worked more closely with him than anyone, "But thou hast fully known my doctrine, manner of life, purpose, faith, longsuffering, charity, patience" (2 Timothy 3:10). He could say this, and Timothy knew it was true.

In our ministry, we've done everything we can to insure that those who lead—as staff or in lay positions—have lives of personal integrity. But when it really comes down to it, personal integrity is a personal matter. Only you know if you are who others believe you to be.

Paul's advice to Timothy is a necessary mandate for anyone in the ministry: "*Take heed unto thyself,* and unto the doctrine; continue in them: for in doing this thou shalt both save thyself, and them that hear thee" (1 Timothy 4:16). In this pithy admonition, we are reminded of those who did *not* take heed to themselves. They may have taken heed to their doctrine or to their reputation, but they failed to take heed to themselves. The ensuing destruction—both for the preacher and for the congregation—has always been tragic.

> Sometimes we need to step back and ask ourselves if we are more hungry for the power of God or for a respected and influential image.

Sometimes we need to step back and ask ourselves if we are more hungry for the power of God or for a respected and influential image. Which consumes the greater portion of our time and attention? Which would we be most willing to forego?

A polished image with tarnished integrity is destined to corrode.

From the pulpit to the pew, moral purity is paramount in the church. If there is open sin in the congregation or hidden sin in the leadership, it must be confronted by holy, godly men. We can't be masters at excusing or covering sin and still expect the revival for which we all pray!

I know something of the pain involved in addressing sin issues. Over the decades, I have had to confront respected leaders and even family members, whom I dearly love, in the spirit of Matthew 18. But as painful as it has been, I have not had peace to invite these men who I know have failed morally to preach in the pulpits of our ministry.

One of the most distressing practices of unhealthy ministries is privately dealing with immorality in church leadership, relieving the man of his public duties...and then recommending the fallen leader to another church! And—this is almost unfathomable—a forward recommendation is sometimes given without even warning the new ministry of the previous failures.[4]

Galatians 6:1–2 speaks of God's graciousness and our Christian responsibility to restore fallen leaders to God, their families, and service

> A polished image with tarnished integrity is destined to corrode.

within the church. Yet, the pastorate should not be one of those areas of service. First Timothy 3 and Titus 1 are both clear that a pastor is to be blameless and the husband of one wife. Brushing sin under the rug and sending a man to another church doesn't answer the "blameless" issue. This unhealthy standard of ministry can only bring unhealthy and corrupt fruit. Ministries that practice such shuffling of sin will tragically corrode from the inside out.

Some sins can and should be dealt with from within the church. Matthew 18 gives clear instructions for handling personal grievances and sin issues. First Corinthians 6 further elaborates that to take such issues to a civil court is defaming to the name of

---

4   This issue was brought up in a Time article regarding Southern Baptist Churches as well. Laura Fitzpatrick, "Top 10 Underreported News Stories... Southern Baptists decide against pedophilia database," November 3, 2008. Retrieved February 28, 2012. http://www.time.com/time/specials/packages/article/0,28804,1855948_1861760_1862212,00.html.

Christ. When a crime is committed, however, it must immediately be reported to civil authorities. Our church policy is that if any person in the church sees a crime take place against a child or receives a report from a child about molestation, he or she must report it to the police. (See Appendix 5.) Indeed, we have reported any abuse of which we've been made aware, including abuse that took place within the homes of children who have ridden our church buses. Church leadership can help to provide counseling in such situations, but we immediately hand criminal matters to the authorities. (See Romans 13:1–4.) There are times when a church worker may not have all the facts, but if a child brings forth an allegation, the laws are clear: it must be reported.

Any form of protecting image over integrity—be it in ignoring sin, hiding crime, or placing more importance on appearance than substance—is pride. It doesn't, as too many have claimed, *protect* the name of Christ; it *tarnishes* His name.

Imbalance #3: Pride in numbers

When people are saved through our churches, God is glorified. And *that* is the greatest privilege of the ministry. For this reason, I keep detailed ministry reports and strive to use the numbers in our ministry to encourage myself and our church members to reach more people for Christ.

But if we shift our focus from God's glory and begin (even subconsciously) to compete with other ministries to be the biggest, greatest, fastest growing, or any other superlative, we cut ourselves off from God's grace. "For we dare not make ourselves of the number, or compare ourselves with some that commend themselves: but they measuring themselves by themselves, and comparing themselves among themselves, are not wise" (2 Corinthians 10:12). A pride in or obsession over numbers can only have detrimental results.

In the history of our movement, I have seen this pride provoke a host of destructive practices and mindsets. These include dishonesty in numbering, viewing needy people as tally marks rather than souls, suspect evangelism methods, relying on programs rather than depending on the Holy Spirit, performance-based acceptance, and, most grievous of all, haughty self-sufficiency.

And then, too, I've seen pride in numbers evoke an unexpected response from young preachers. Wanting to be a pastor of a growing church and frustrated over their lack of numeric increase, they are sometimes lured to change ministry affiliations. Other groups may convince such pastors that the reasons behind their "lack of success" are archaic methods (such as door-to-door soulwinning) and "legalistic" philosophies (such as a pursuit of holiness). In reality, the size of their church may not be a sign of weakness at all. It may be that they are on the right track

> When we take pride in numbers, we redefine God's definition of success.

and God is bringing them through a season of personal growth; it may be they serve in a smaller community; or it may be indeed that they are not being diligent in personal outreach and hands-on discipleship.

Regardless of the cause, I've watched too many young men shift ministry philosophies and doctrine in their quest for "success." These pastors are often disappointed further as they discover that their attendances are not dramatically affected and they are now grappling with compromise. Unfortunately, the damage has already been done.

When we take pride in numbers, we redefine *God's* definition of success. God is not as interested in the size of our churches as He is in our faithfulness to His truth. I praise God for every soul saved here in Lancaster, California, and in every other ministry around the world. But I dare not take pride in any soul saved by the grace of God flowing through my, or my church family's, obedience.

Imbalance #4: Pride in men

Twenty years ago, in a message at a conference of Christian leaders, I preached from 1 Corinthians 3 about the carnality of divisions such as "I am of Paul" or "I am of Apollos." I addressed servant leadership as opposed to prideful cliques among Baptists. Tragically, I don't believe many of the men present had a clue that the message addressed their current relationships and philosophies. It was as if the widespread prevalence of pride in men had so blinded them that they were not able to see the forest for the trees.

As Christians, our allegiance is solely to the Lord Jesus Christ, and our mission is to point others to Him. Why, then, do we deteriorate into divisions over personalities, institutions, and preferences? Why do we glory—take pride—in who we know, where we went to school, or which fundamental leader we follow? Why do we write mass letters and feisty blogs about *men?*

In rebuking the church for allowing division over personalities, Paul cut right to the root: "are ye not carnal?" (1 Corinthians 3:4). Co-laborers in the Lord, Paul and Apollos preached the same gospel with the same doctrine. Yet, some in the church felt compelled to choose sides. And, after all these years and even with the Scriptures to guide us, we haven't changed. Now, just as then, every time we pride ourselves in our associations with men, institutions, or issues, we grieve the only One who grants true empowerment—the Holy Spirit of God.

We should thank God for good men and institutions, but they should not become the test of our fellowship. Who we know, where we went to school, what conferences we attend, and similar marks of distinction should have little impact on the greater focus of Who we are striving together to make known.

Imbalance #5: Pride in standards

Truthfully, everyone has some standards of living—even if they are extremely liberal standards. Everyone draws a line *somewhere*. Standards drawn from biblical principles are essential in practicing the doctrines of holiness and purity.

One of the distinctives of the independent Baptist movement and any Christ-honoring group has been a commitment to holiness and a practice of separating from the world. This distinctive is biblically rooted. Reflective of the nature of God, it is pleasing to the Lord. In fact, I believe that a willingness to obey the command "Love not the world" (1 John 2:15) is one of the reasons God has blessed and entrusted us with the continuing growth of new Christians. A culture that promotes holiness and the work of the Holy Spirit is a virtual greenhouse for Christian growth!

So I'm not in any way, shape, or form bashing standards. (I believe in them; ask our West Coast Baptist College students.) But I am repudiating *pride* in standards. If we focus on standards, there is a temptation to glory in our standards, sometimes even to the neglect of deeper heart issues. This problem is dealt with throughout the book of Galatians but is often overlooked by men who do not rightly divide such books.

Jesus Himself dealt with the issue of pride in standards repeatedly, and it was always in relation to the hypocrisy it evokes in spiritual leaders. In Matthew 23, He specifically differentiated between the authority of the Word of God and the authority of imposed standards.

> Then spake Jesus to the multitude, and to his disciples, Saying, The scribes and the Pharisees sit in Moses' seat: All therefore whatsoever they bid you observe, that observe and do; but do not ye after their works: for they say, and do not. For they bind heavy burdens and grievous to be borne, and lay them on men's shoulders; but they themselves will not move them with one of their fingers.—MATTHEW 23:1–4

"Moses' seat" refers to the spiritual office of the scribes and Pharisees. They were responsible to declare and teach the law of Moses. Jesus made it clear that when a spiritual leader sits "in Moses' seat"—or declares the Word of God to us—we are to "observe and do"—obey. But when a spiritual leader is imposing his own standards *as if it were equal to God's Word,* we are not obligated to follow it. This is pride in standards—leaders using their office to impose extra-biblical and burdensome rules.

As the well-known saying goes, "Rules without relationships breed rebellion." The most vital relationship in the heart of a believer is with his Lord. A list of rules without a walk with God will never culminate toward a Christ-honoring life.[5]

Romans 13:14 does teach us to make no provision for fleshly lusts, but it does so with the instruction, "Put ye on the Lord Jesus Christ." We must understand and teach the believer's relationship with Christ as a foundation for pleasing Him in areas of holy living. I recently spoke with a young pastor who said he felt the church he was raised in put an emphasis on teaching Christians to "put on Christianity" (through standards without a close relationship with Christ) rather than to "put on Christ" (through a heart and life transformed by God's Spirit working through His Word).

When our litmus test for either the maturity of a young Christian or our ability to receive from an older Christian *begins* with how they dress or what music they listen to rather than how their hearts are developing in grace or the fruit of the Spirit in their lives, we have elevated standards above grace.

Before you say it, I already know: growth in grace will result in outward change. That's absolutely true, and I believe it so strongly that I wrote an entire book about it.[6] Holiness is a vital doctrine, and modesty is clearly a biblical component of that doctrine. Spiritual music is essential to spiritual growth.

But God's *emphasis* is still on the heart.[7] And if *our* emphasis is on the heart, we will care more about a person's process of growth than his or her external signs of growth. We will also be less prone to assume that our own hearts are pure solely because our standards are high.

---

5   Matthew 23:23
6   *Grace for Godly Living*, Striving Together Publications, 2005.
7   Proverbs 4:23

Only through obedience to the instruction of 2 Corinthians 10:17 will we free ourselves from this sinful boasting in standards: "But he that glorieth, let him glory in the Lord." Our focus and our joy must always be rooted in Jesus. If a standard is based upon a biblical conviction and it helps us to be more Christlike, then all the glory should go to Christ. When, however, we are proud of ourselves and our standards, we glorify ourselves—is that less sinful than the immodesty or "worldliness" of the fellow Christian we have placed under our microscope?

Imbalance #6: Little or no accountability within leadership

As the media has uncovered tragic stories of abuse in "IFB" churches, reporters repeatedly cite the "independent" status of the church as a common component to the abuse. They mistakenly assume that since the church has no denominational board to which the pastor must give an account, crime is more easily hidden and perpetuated than it is within denominations.

This accusation narrowly misses the truth. It's correct that accountability is key, but there's a world of difference between what the reporters think and what needs to change.

The autonomy of the local church is a Bible doctrine, and God certainly didn't establish doctrines that would endanger those who are vulnerable. Thus, the independent status isn't the problem at all; the non-accountability status is. And accountability is a choice that *every* leader—in or out of a denomination—must personally make.

A higher structure of authority within the Catholic church did not prevent the abuse that came to light several years ago,[8] including

---

8   "Timeline: US Church Sex Scandal," BBC News, September 7, 2007, http://news.bbc.co.uk/2/hi/americas/3872499 stm.

repeated offences by priests shuffled from one parish to another to avoid legal actions.[9] Nor did it prevent the recently documented abuse by a respected leader within the Jewish community.[10] Even in the secular field, abuse and cover-ups take place on a regular basis. Penn State faced its own scandal,[11] and just this week, I read an article singling out the Boy Scouts as being covert in their responses to known

> Accountability
> is a choice that
> every leader must
> personally make.

abuse.[12] I don't cite these examples to excuse any abuse that has taken place in any ministry; I simply point out that ties to an outside system of hierarchy do not prevent abuse in any organization.

Sin will always find the darkest corner from which to work. Spiritual, physical, and sexual abuse is not bound to one group or church. But it does lurk in lives and systems that shy away from accountability.

Every spiritual leader, including the senior pastor, needs personal accountability. Personally, I have chosen to gather a team of godly men with whom I meet (sometimes on the phone, but

---

9   "Sex abuse victim accuses Catholic church of fraud," USA Today, June 29, 2010, http://usatoday30.usatoday.com/news/religion/2010–06–24-fraud23_ST_N.htm.

10   Rande Iaboni, "Chemical Thrown on Rabbi Who Advocated for Abuse Victims," CNN, December 12, 2012, http://religion.blogs.cnn.com/2012/12/12/chemical-thrown-on-rabbi-who-advocated-for-abuse-victims-lawyer-says/.

11   Susan Candiotti, Josh Levs, and David Ariosto, "Penn State leaders disregarded victims, 'empowered' Sandusky, review finds," CNN, July 12, 2012, http://www.cnn.com/2012–07–12/us/pennsylvania-penn-state-investigation.

12   Kim Christensen, "Boy Scouts have history of laying blame on victim," Los Angeles Times, December 25, 2012, http://m.startribune.com/news/?id=184776271&c=y.

often in person) on a regular basis for accountability. These men know they have access into every area of my life—and they take the access. They ask me probing questions regarding my walk with the Lord, family time, reading, and thoughts; and they do not hesitate to point out imbalances they see developing in any area of my life. I thank God for these men. I know myself, and I know that I need them.

The men that I have chosen have had the following distinguishing characteristics:

1. More mature than I am in ministry years
2. Faithful in doctrinal integrity
3. Have testimonies of personal holiness
4. Love their wives and families
5. Have families who love Jesus
6. Love me enough to be honest with me
7. Love the local church

If accountability is necessary in our personal lives, it is also necessary to the function and operations of the church. For the testimony of Christ and the protection of those in our care, every person involved in church ministry—paid or volunteer— must be willing to adhere to a high standard of integrity in service. This includes exercising discernment and prudence as well as a commitment to follow ministry policies designed for everyone's protection. (See Appendix 5.)

Additionally, leadership in the church needs vigilant accountability in matters of finances and ministry propriety. Not only should a pastor, staff, and deacons hold one another accountable in these matters from within, but outside audits add an additional level of security. Our church and ministry finances are audited annually by an outside CPA firm, and our internal control system involves healthy checks and balances for lay workers and staff alike.

I challenge you, as a spiritual leader, to commit to openness and accountability in every area of your life. Do not pridefully lift yourself above the concern of others. Remain approachable and sincere with good, godly men.

Imbalance #7: Unbiblical preaching

It is a tremendous responsibility to preach the powerful, life-changing Word of God. "For the word of God is quick [living], and powerful, and sharper than any twoedged sword, piercing even to the dividing asunder of soul and spirit, and of the joints and marrow, and is a discerner of the thoughts and intents of the heart" (Hebrews 4:12).

With such a sword at our disposal, why do we neglect it, filling our sermons with stories instead of with Scripture? Illustrations can be wonderful tools to illustrate truth. (Spurgeon said, "A sermon without illustrations is like a room without windows."[13]) But preaching that, as a norm, ignores the scriptural context, support verses and their contexts, word definitions, historical backgrounds, and accurate applications isn't rightly dividing the Word of truth (2 Timothy 2:15). It turns us into storytellers rather than preachers.

And what about preaching that declares opinions as gospel truth? Paul commanded Timothy, "Preach *the word;* be instant in

---

13   Charles Haddon Spurgeon, Mrs. Susannah Spurgeon, and W. J. Harrald, *The Autobiography of Charles H. Spurgeon: 1856–1878* (Fleming H. Revell Company, 1899), 63.

season, out of season; reprove, rebuke, exhort with all longsuffering and doctrine" (2 Timothy 4:2). One of the most tragic mistakes we make is when we elevate personal opinions to a doctrinal level. We all have opinions, but if we share them from the pulpit or from our position as a spiritual leader, we should be careful to differentiate between preferences and God's Word. I find that people—church members and younger preachers alike—generally respect and appreciate the clarification. Explaining the philosophy behind a preference while admitting that it is indeed a preference doesn't make the listeners less likely to hold a similar position. If anything, it increases their respect for the leader who explains, and it strengthens their resolve to follow in the same.

> One of the most tragic mistakes we make is when we elevate personal opinions to a doctrinal level.

Another expression of unbiblical preaching is using a shock effect to capture audience attention through inserting profanity or sexual innuendoes into a sermon. Because of our sacred responsibility as preachers of God's Word, vulgar or offensive language has no place in the pulpit. Paul twice warned Timothy of "profane and vain babblings" (1 Timothy 6:20; 2 Timothy 2:16), instructing him to avoid and shun them because they increase ungodliness. (They may increase audience attention, but it is at the cost of decreasing audience purity.) In both of these verses the word *profane* is translated from the Greek word βέβηλος, an adjective used to describe that which is unhallowed, ungodly, or common. I think it would be safe to say that these verses preclude the use of both profanity and base language. Propriety in speech elevates purity in lives.

Nothing can replace the contextual, expository preaching of God's Word. I occasionally preach topical sermons, but even in them I strive to include dozens of verses. Stories and illustrations are helpful, but we must always remember that it is the Word of God itself that changes the heart.

Imbalance #8: Lack of grace

God's grace is dynamic. It is active, powerful, vigorous. It changes lives. I know, because it changed (and continues to change) mine; and for the past twenty-seven years, I've watched it change the lives of the people I'm privileged to pastor.

An emphasis on grace is indispensable for biblical ministry. We are saved by grace (Ephesians 2:8–9). We are changed into Christ's likeness by grace (2 Corinthians 3:18). We endure trials by grace (2 Corinthians 12:9). We give by grace (2 Corinthians 8:6–8). We communicate spiritually by grace (Colossians 4:6). No true Christian growth can develop apart from grace (Philippians 2:13).

But unbalanced ministries overlook the powerful motivator of grace, instead motivating or exerting control through the lesser substitutes of guilt or fear. A lack of grace was probably one of my heaviest imbalances in early years of ministry. As I have grown in grace (and prayerfully continue growing), God has centered our ministry more firmly in grace. It is the joy of my life to have part in nurturing the growth in grace of God's people.

Graceless spiritual leaders manifest pride through shortness with others, lack of mercy, a caustic spirit, and a condemning attitude. Grace-filled leaders manifest graciousness through personal humility, patience with growing Christians, and a passion to connect people—not to an outer conformity—but to the dynamic grace of God that will change their lives from the inside out.

> Unbalanced ministries overlook the powerful motivator of grace.

As spiritual leaders, we have been entrusted with the boundless grace of God. Our lives and our ministries are to be showcases that illuminate God's grace. How tragic, then, when a local church and/or its spiritual leadership preach salvation by grace but live and lead in a manner that denies grace. What a confusing imbalance!

Imbalance #9: Pride in position

A sure sign of a grace-filled, humble spiritual leader is one who is grateful for the truth, rather than proud of knowing it. When any person, church, or group takes pride in itself, God will resist that person, church, or group. Sooner or later, He will expose them for who they are apart from His grace and remove His blessing. (We'll look at this issue in more depth in chapter 7.)

As we noted in chapter 3, the independent fundamental Baptist movement had humble beginnings. God greatly blessed these men who had a firm commitment to principle. But tragically, as God's blessings rose on this humble movement, hearts lifted with the successes. As the movement gained influence, some leaders seemed to gain belligerence.

We should be thankful to take our place in a long legacy of men who have studied God's Word for truth and made Bible convictions their rule for faith and practice. But we dare not become prideful in this position. After all, we are what we are only by God's grace.[14]

Imbalance #10: Misplaced identity

At the heart of most pride problems is a works-based identity. Do we value ourselves based on the number of hours we worked or the number of people in our Sunday school class? If so, we will be on a fruitless and frustrating treadmill seeking for approval that we will never fully find.

If we believe that God's blessing is determined by our Christian service, we are under the weight of self-reliance. We were not made to shoulder this load, and we will never be successful at carrying it for very long. In our grasp for significance, we miss delighting in the Father alone and knowing that He delights in us.

I believe that Scripture teaches my behavior can please or displease Christ,[15] but the blessings of God are always because of His grace. When my identity is found in my performance rather than His grace, I can develop an unscriptural sense of worth that is not based on my new birth in Christ.

Where do we find our worth and acceptance? Ephesians 1:6 provides the welcome answer: "He hath made us accepted in the beloved." Period. Not "accepted in the Beloved plus our performance." Accepted in Jesus.

Of course, any Christian who believes in eternal security teaches that *salvation* is not based on service for Christ. But the identity issue goes beyond salvation. What is our identity as a saved

14   1 Corinthians 15:10
15   2 Timothy 2:4

follower of Christ based on—God's love, or approval through conformity or service? Balanced ministries are led by Christians who have embraced their identity in Christ. These servant leaders then invest their lives in teaching others to likewise serve from the security of God's unearned love.

Incidentally, if you think this imbalance is easy to correct, I'd like to get some tips from you! My flesh is bent on seeking approval for what I *do*. (Most of us preachers hope our wife compliments the message on the way to Sunday lunch!) It's a lifelong journey to continually mortify the flesh and rest in who I am in Christ.

FOR THE SAKE OF REVIVAL

If there is one word that encapsulates what we need today it is *revival*.

Our nation needs revival. Our churches need revival. Our leaders need revival. *I* need revival. *You* need revival.

With such a desperate need, you'd think we'd do anything to obtain it, right?

The condition for revival is actually quite simple, and it is contained in one of the most well-known verses of the Old Testament:

> If my people, which are called by my name, shall humble themselves, and pray, and seek my face, and turn from their wicked ways; then will I hear from heaven, and will forgive their sin, and will heal their land.
> —2 CHRONICLES 7:14

That's it! If we will humble ourselves, pray, seek God's face, and turn from our sin, He will send revival.

So…why don't we have revival?

Perhaps we are too proud?

Somehow we independent Baptists seem to have come to believe that our degree of *rightness*—right doctrine, right standards, right music, right preaching—lays the strongest claim for God to use us. As vital as true doctrine and biblical practices are, these are not what opens our ministries to God's power.

James 4:6 says it in black and white: "God resisteth the proud, but giveth grace unto the humble."

It's a promise. God *always* humbles the proud and elevates the humble.

Human pride is such an affront to God that even if we are doing a good thing—in pride—God *will* resist our efforts. Even if our doctrine is right and our methods are biblical, if we are operating from a heart of pride, we can prepare to find our efforts eventually brought to nothing. Dr. John Goetsch has said, "God doesn't share His glory with anybody. He will not send revival until He can trust us with one."[16]

Frankly, God doesn't *have* to use us. Throughout history, He's used all kinds of people and groups to further His work. Some have even had errors in their doctrine, methods, or philosophies, and yet God has used them. For instance, some of the

> "God doesn't share His glory with anybody. He will not send revival until He can trust us with one."
>
> —Dr. John Goetsch

---

16   John Goetsch, *Twenty-First Century Revival: Is it Possible?* (Striving Together Publications, 2007), 51.

preachers of the First or Second Great Awakenings were not men whom I would likely invite as guest speakers at Lancaster Baptist Church. In many cases, they were not Baptist and had different doctrinal persuasions in relation to the local church, baptism, eternal security, etc. And yet, surprisingly enough by our thinking, God greatly used these men! It was through their sermons that the Holy Spirit ignited nationwide revival.

God is not limited in who He will use. He doesn't have to use either you or me! He primarily seeks to use those who have humble, contrite hearts.

STEP BACKSTAGE A MOMENT

Each of us has a public life and a private life. In ministry, our public life is very public. Some call it a fishbowl. For a moment, though, think of it as a front stage.[17]

On the front stage, you minister to others. You preach, sing, lead, counsel, study, administrate, etc. In fact, there's so much to be done on the front stage that it's easy to forget or neglect the backstage.

But you do have a backstage. Behind the curtain, you have the part of your life that only God, your family, and anyone to whom you've given entrance is familiar with. Back here is where you pray, meditate, read and study God's Word, love your wife, invest in your children. Or where you don't.

The front stage is public. The backstage is personal.

---

17   I've heard this illustration through the years, but it most recently stood out to me as I read Lance Witt's book *Replenish: Leading from a Healthy Soul* (Baker Books, 2011), 23–24.

The front stage is exciting. The backstage is essential.

The front stage is presentation. The backstage is preparation.

Without the backstage, the front stage won't produce well for very long. Neglect it, and your front stage audience will trickle away. They won't understand what has happened to you. *You* may not understand what has happened to you.

It's really quite simple. You forgot to spend time backstage.

> We must have a backstage life.

If we as independent Baptists are to correct the imbalances of the past and achieve victories for God's glory in the future, if we are to lead well and to lead biblically, if we are to be godly—we must have a backstage life. We must give attention to the hidden areas of our soul and humbly seek God's grace to lead with integrity.

IN PURSUIT OF BALANCE

To minister with a balance of grace and truth is a delicate journey. And along that passage, as we make it our driving purpose to know Christ, we learn to serve like Him—full of grace and truth.

Any of these ten imbalances—and especially the pride that drives them—can creep up on us with such stealth as to make the imbalance imperceptible in the beginning. But, oh, what damage it will work! For this reason, it is vital that we daily, constantly, look to the Holy Spirit for conviction, cleansing, and power!

I pray that those who carry the name of Christ, and specifically those who call themselves independent Baptists, will make Christ their goal as they serve with humility and personal purity. In the future, some of us may refer to ourselves as "biblical Baptists" or "unaffiliated Baptists," but more important than the descriptive adjectives we choose is that we return to the New Testament model of servant leadership, focused evangelism, and purposed discipleship.

I pray for days of greater camaraderie among men who understand, like leaders of yesteryear, that independent pastors can be different in minor opinions but still be brothers praying for revival and planting churches. I pray that all of us will turn from whatever glory we may perceive in our position (doctrinal or practical) and redirect every beam of focus on Christ alone. May we serve in His church with integrity and humility that brings glory to His name.

Be Grace Givers

Take a trip with me back to the 1960s.

Externally, America was engaged in the Vietnam war. Internally, the nation wrestled over the Civil Rights movement. In the second half of the decade, the younger generation revolted against cultural norms and launched the hippie movement. Teenagers dropped out of school, packed their bags in their Volkswagens, and migrated to the coasts to get high on LSD and marijuana.

Throughout this decade of change, independent fundamental Baptists were known for separating themselves from the world's culture. Baptist preachers weren't shy about denouncing the loose, licentious lifestyle of the day—or anything that resembled it. They boldly thundered against hippie hair on men, immodest clothing on women, and anything that resembled worldly lifestyles. Newly saved Christians who were reached through independent Baptist churches quickly cut their hair, burned their rock records, and purchased a Scofield Reference Bible.

Now, let's move further back in time. Let's visit the conservative Christians of the eighteenth century and listen to a respected preacher address separation in matters of women's attire:

> Let your dress be cheap as well as plain. Otherwise you do but trifle with God and me, and your own souls. I pray, let there be no costly silks among you, how grave soever they may be. Let there be no Quaker linen; proverbially so called, for their exquisite fineness: no Brussels lace, no elephantine hats or bonnets, those scandals of female modesty. Be all of a piece, dressed from head to foot, as persons professing godliness: professing to do every thing, small and great, with the single view of pleasing God.—JOHN WESLEY[1]

Sort of jolting, isn't it? Until I read Wesley's sermon this past summer, I had never considered the ungodliness of two-piece outfits on women. Not even once.

Have you ever wondered why, as independent fundamental Baptists, we insist on the definitions of modesty from the 1960s but not from the 1700s? The preachers in both of these eras had biblical principles upon which they based these standards. Wesley could have cited 1 Timothy 2:9 and Titus 2:5. But you and I don't read those verses today and come to the same conclusions as Wesley.

The truth is, in a case like this, the context of applying biblical principles does shift. In the 1960s, preachers addressed facial hair

---

1   John Wesley, *Sermons on Several Occasions, Vol. II*, (Nelson & Phillips, 1788), 264–265.

on men from Romans 12:2: "And be not conformed to this world...."
But I don't read this passage today and see the same connection—
primarily because our culture has shifted. A well-groomed beard is
no longer seen as identification with rebellion. (If you don't believe
me, try telling a new convert in his thirties that he should shave his
beard so he is not identified as a hippie. He will wonder what planet
you came from!)

While we do not advocate changing true biblical convictions
with the culture, it is important that we simply ask, how do we, as
biblical Baptists, respond to those in our own circles of fellowship
who believe the same biblical principles we do, but have slightly
different standards?

ROMANS 14

The first-century church grappled with issues of principles and
standards early on—especially in the matter of meat offered to
idols. To a twenty-first-century Christian, their heated debates over
meat seem illogical and easily resolved. But I doubt any American
can fully grasp the significance of the collision of cultures taking
place within the early church.

Jews—God's chosen people with devout obedience to His law,
plus a few of their own tagged on for good measure—struggled to
understand how a regenerate man could feel the liberty to disregard
the law of Moses.

Gentiles—men and women steeped in generations of idolatry
and superstition—reveled in the freedom of the gospel. They
wondered how Jews could be so insistent on following the rituals
of an empty religion.

Mature Christians of either background grew in grace and gained confidence in walking in the liberty brought by the Holy Spirit. But even as they exercised their liberty, they were sure to offend young Christians of either Jewish or Gentile backgrounds.

With that background, it's not difficult to see how there could have been a few conflicts of standards in the early churches!

Some of the Christians believed they could eat meat that had been offered to idols with complete freedom of conscience. But other Christians—those newer in the Lord and more recently connected to the heathen sacrifices—felt they were violating their consciences by eating the meat.

Paul settled the matter clearly in both Romans 14 and 1 Corinthians 8. From these passages, we learn how to respond to Christians who embrace slightly different standards than we do.

WHY ROMANS 14 MATTERS TODAY

Biblical Baptist churches have a long heritage of defending the truth and caring deeply about personal holiness.

We Baptists know that we are called to be a peculiar people, and we delight in identifying ourselves with our God. First Peter 2:9 declares, "But ye are a chosen generation, a royal priesthood, an holy nation, a peculiar people; that ye should shew forth the praises of him who hath called you out of darkness into his marvellous light."

As with many words, the definition of *peculiar* has shifted and expanded over time. In seventeenth-century English as well as in biblical Greek, the word referred to possession, especially to identifying that which characteristically belonged to a person or group. For instance, a person might say, "He has a peculiar preaching style." While today, they would probably be trying to gently say that his preaching style is strange, four hundred years ago, they would have meant that his preaching style was unique to him—it could easily be identified as his.

Unfortunately, many of our independent Baptist brethren use the newer definition of *peculiar*—strange. In some cases, they've taken that to the extreme of being flat out weird. Some have elevated differences and idiosyncrasies to the point of a test of fellowship.

When Peter penned 1 Peter 2:9, he wasn't speaking of preserving a culture from the earlier days of fundamentalism. Nor was he speaking of shunning the cultural taboos of past generations. He was admonishing his readers to live a lifestyle that clearly proclaimed their allegiance to the God who owned them.

Many younger independent Baptists know "the standards," but tragically not the Bible passages or principles from which they are drawn. A **command** is obvious. It is a spelled-out instruction in the Word of God. From that command, we see a **principle.** Bible principles allow us to address the specific issues of life that are addressed in a larger sense in Scripture. Finally, from a principle, we develop **standards** that bring the original command into direct contact with our daily living.[2]

The timeless nature of God's Word means that every command applies with equal obligation to each generation of Christians. Its principles do not waver, but are broad enough to reach every culture and long enough to hold true through the millennia. The

---

2   For a more detailed explanation of how principles develop standards, see article "The Basis for Biblical Standards" by Dr. R. B. Ouellette at http://ministry127.com/pastoral-leadership/the-basis-for-biblical-standards. Published July 24, 2012.

standards we draw from its pages may vary slightly among godly people, but they hold us to the unchanging bedrock of truth.

WHEN TO STAND AND WHEN TO BE GRACIOUS

As a pastor and, more importantly, as a Christian, I believe in the doctrine of holiness—that God is holy and that we are to be holy.[3] I believe in the biblical principles that support holiness such as modesty, distinction between men and women, separation from worldliness, and conservative worship. Furthermore, I personally enjoy fellowship with those who likewise embrace these principles.

> The timeless nature of God's Word means that every command applies with equal obligation to each generation of Christians.

But I don't believe in ostracizing people who don't practice every principle exactly the way I do. I have no intention of moving to "the left." But I have every intention of being gracious toward people who aren't exactly like me.

Let me explain with a reasonably familiar scenario: A godly, spiritually minded Christian listens to a special group in church. They happen to sing a song that has not been sung in this particular church before. The seated Christian is uncomfortable—the song is unfamiliar, and he's not sure he likes it. He listens carefully to the

---

words. Nothing wrong there—they are doctrinal and exalt Christ. He pays close attention to the music. Nothing wrong there either— it is melodious with supporting harmony and a gently supporting rhythm. Sure, he could find a note he doesn't care for or a vocal technique that isn't his preference. But to be honest, he could have found those last week when the same group sang "Amazing Grace." It didn't bother him then. So why is he uncomfortable now? In all honesty, the only "sin" of the song is that it is unfamiliar.

We could walk through a similar scenario in other areas of choice—women's attire, manger scenes in the church, the use of technology, facial hair on men, and more—actually, *lots* more. Because Scripture applies to every area of life, these topics are addressed by principle within the pages of God's Word. But you would be hard pressed to find a chapter and verse that draws a definitive line between the black and the white here. There are godly men who stand on different sides of every one of these issues.

When a man believes he has a biblical conviction regarding a teaching or practice, he should say so and should share the scriptural support for his conviction. But where a true preference is involved, he should be clear on this as well. Sometimes, we might even brand good ministries as "worldly" because we are unwilling to give fellow brothers in Christ space to have personal preferences[4] or differences.

This is where Romans 14 comes into play. This chapter primarily deals with issues of ceremonial law, not moral issues. In

---

4   My friend, Dr. Dave Hardy, cautions concerning the use of the word
     preference lest we begin using it to de-emphasize doctrine, calling essentials
     "non-essentials." As I use the word in this chapter, however, I refer to areas
     which are not specifically addressed in Scripture in which godly leaders who
     believe the same doctrine and principles have slight differences in practice.

fact, verse 17 says, "For the kingdom of God is not meat and drink; but righteousness, and peace, and joy in the Holy Ghost." Biblically, there is no room for us to differ on moral issues. (Adultery, for instance, is always wrong.) So Romans 14 doesn't give room to cross the clear line drawn by Scripture, but this chapter does give us principles for when and how we differ with our brother where no moral principle has been violated.

In this chapter, God guides us through the troubling issues of nonconformity within our ranks. It gives us a biblical perspective of understanding those who interpret Scripture and culture a little bit differently than we do. Most importantly, it provides us with seven principles on how to have unity where there are differences in certain practices.

Principle #1: Give grace

> Him that is weak in the faith receive ye, but not to doubtful disputations. For one believeth that he may eat all things: another, who is weak, eateth herbs. Let not him that eateth despise him that eateth not; and let not him which eateth not judge him that eateth: for God hath received him. Who art thou that judgest another man's servant? to his own master he standeth or falleth. Yea, he shall be holden up: for God is able to make him stand.—ROMANS 14:1–4

Notice especially verse 3. Although originally penned to address different issues than we face today, its principle is applicable and needed in this hour: "Let not him that eateth despise him that eateth not; and let not him which eateth not judge him that eateth: for God hath received him."

Allow that to sink in: God has received him.

Who am I to condemn another believer—especially over areas on which we agree in principle but vary in practice—when God has received him?

The word *despise* here means "regard with contempt." I have seen independent Baptists leaders whose conduct exactly matched this description. Over slight differences of practice, I've watched men treat each other very poorly.

In Warren Wiersbe's commentary on Romans 14, he noted that when Christian radio broadcasting was just becoming a reality, many Christians were against it. They even had a chapter and verse—Ephesians 2:2, which identifies Satan as "the prince of the power of the air."[5] Wiersbe said that good people rebuked him for going on the air because of this concern.

I can understand an independent Baptist having leadership requirements in the church, but I do not support making all my standards a test of fellowship with others. Anytime we judge one another over minor issues, we reveal the pettiness of our own hearts; and we usually reveal our lack of understanding regarding the Bible principle we are so adamantly defending.

> Anytime we judge one another over minor issues, we reveal the pettiness of our own hearts.

5   Warren Wiersbe, *The Bible Exposition Commentary: New Testament: Volume 1* (David C. Cook, 2003), 559.

Every clear teaching of the Word of God should be honored. But honesty demands any thinking Christian to acknowledge that really good people will have differences of opinion. God gives them grace; we should as well.

For spiritual leaders who are tired of bickering over differences in the name of doctrine, Romans 14 holds good news: we can be faithful to the truth and yet be gracious to those who live out the truth differently than we do. The kindness and humility commanded in this passage is a rebuke to the harshness and pride which has too often held sway among fundamental Baptist leaders.

Principle #2: Show kindness

> But why dost thou judge thy brother? or why dost thou set at nought thy brother? for we shall all stand before the judgment seat of Christ.—ROMANS 14:10

A few years ago, Terrie and I visited Greece and retraced some of Paul's footsteps. In Corinth, I saw a bema seat—the judgment seat. There amid the broken remains of ancient Corinth stands part of the remnants of the old stone platform which the bema seat topped. The bema was the place where the judges stood at the athletic games and from which they pronounced the victor.

With a picture of the bema in his mind, Paul reminded the Corinthian believers, "For we must all appear before the judgment seat of Christ; that every one may receive the things done in his body, according to that he hath done, whether it be good or bad" (2 Corinthians 5:10).

It was this seat to which Paul referred in Romans 14:10. By calling to mind the judgment seat of Christ—that place where only the Judge has a say on the race's competitors—Paul is reminding us that it is not our place to make a judgment call on the worth of another believer. What authority do I have to judge my brother or to set him at naught (count him as nothing)? It's simply not my place.

When we set each other at naught because of differences in opinion or preference, we take on God's job.

If my brother has a slight variance in his music standard,[6] if he prefers to have no Christmas decorations while I enjoy a church nativity scene, if he has a slightly different interpretation of what he believes is most modest, if he believes he should not own a television while I watch the evening news, if he…it doesn't matter! I don't have to embrace his personal convictions—to the right or left—as my own. But neither do I need to castigate him to keep my standing before God. I simply show kindness and mind my own business. God allows for differences; why should I be less kind than the Judge?

Principle #3: Have faith

> One man esteemeth one day above another: another esteemeth every day alike. Let every man be fully persuaded in his own mind….And he that doubteth is damned if he eat, because he eateth not of faith: for whatsoever is not of faith is sin.—ROMANS 14:5, 23

---

6   Please do not confuse this statement for an endorsement of Christian rock or the CCM (Christian Contemporary Music) movement as a whole. Music is not amoral! I believe, however, we are too quick to judge others on the basis of slight differences in music selection or vocal techniques within the realm of conservative, Christ-honoring music and spiritual songs.

The Christian life is to be lived by faith.[7] Faith is the foundation from which we please God.[8] This is why when Paul addressed this issue of standards in Romans 14, he brought it back to the center point of faith: "Let every man be fully persuaded in his own mind... whatsoever is not of faith is sin." I don't know how Paul could have been more plain in pointing out the real issue. Matters of personal standards are matters of personal faith developed with the leading of the Holy Spirit and the Word of God.

Some fundamental churches have unintentionally created a spirit of performance-based acceptance—and the performance usually relates to standards or soulwinning productivity. It grieves me to know that churches across the nation that have cultivated this environment have led thousands of dear Christians to believe they were not truly loved and accepted if they could not meet every rule (or at least discern and meet those rules which the church leaders considered the most important).

I know enough leaders to know that this culture of performance-based acceptance has generally been created unintentionally and often with the leaders being unaware of its deep-rooted existence. In some cases, the leader's oblivion has been due to insecurities in his own heart. In other cases, it has been a failure to thoroughly evaluate the methods he's been handed in conferences and from colleges and sift the carnal from the spiritual. I understand the need for leadership requirements in our churches, but these requirements and their accompanying positions of service should not be the basis for receiving love and acceptance in the church.

---

7   2 Corinthians 5:7
8   Hebrews 11:6

I pray that biblical Baptists return to a place of respecting the consciences of others while encouraging younger Christians to seriously and prayerfully make decisions in faith that will guide them to Christlikeness.

An idea has seeped into fundamentalism that a Christian's level of discipleship and spirituality can be determined by his number of personal standards. In other words, the more standards you have, the more spiritual you are. Romans 14 emphatically forbids this spirit. In fact, in this passage it was the weaker brother who needed more standards, not the stronger brother.

God has created us with a free will to yield to and follow His Holy Spirit. In developing standards, some independent Baptists take an approach by faith in areas where I cannot see the leading of the Lord. This may seem confusing, but God did not create us to be robots who are programmed, but Christians who are led by His Word and His Spirit.

When it comes to matters of the conscience we, as spiritual leaders, are not to program the consciences of others. Of course, as spiritual leaders, we teach the truths of Scripture, and we make strong impressions on our children and young believers. But we must emphasize to them the importance of making decisions of faith under the leadership of the Holy Spirit.

In the end, I can only have faith for me, and you can only have faith for you. (This truth, in fact, directly relates to one of our Baptist distinctives—individual soul liberty.) I guess that puts us back to where we started—we need to give grace toward each other.

Principle #4: Be discerning

Perhaps one reason those of us who lead in local churches[9] have struggled with the principles of Romans 14 is because we are genuinely concerned for the young Christians among us. It seems safer to trust standards rather than trust an immature believer to have the discernment necessary for his protection. We know how deceptive the human heart can be, and we know discernment takes time to develop.

Paul was not oblivious to these concerns. He loved young Christians with a parental willingness to spend and be spent to encourage just a little growth in their lives. Thus, even as Paul instructed the Roman believers to personally seek the Lord in matters of personal standards, he added a reminder of the gravity of their choices:

> But why dost thou judge thy brother? or why dost thou set at nought thy brother? for we shall all stand before the judgment seat of Christ. For it is written, As I live, saith the Lord, every knee shall bow to me, and every tongue shall confess to God. So then every one of us shall give account of himself to God.—ROMANS 14:10–12

Can you with a clear conscience believe that you can stand before Christ and not be ashamed for putting up a Christmas tree? If not, then don't do it. If yes, enjoy it. Can you stand before Christ

---

9   Obviously, these principles do not negate a parent's responsibility to enforce rules for minors in their home, nor an institution's (such as a Christian school or Bible college) need to regulate guidelines and personal habits for the benefit of everyone's growth and safety. Even many public schools in California have found it necessary to have standardized school uniforms because of gang problems.

with a television sitting in your living room? That's not for me to decide. It is, however, for you to decide. And as you decide, you must have full confidence that you will be able to stand unashamed at the judgment seat of Christ.

The phrase "as unto the Lord," used in verse 6 of Romans 14 reminds us that we are to build our convictions on pleasing the Lord rather than on pleasing our flesh.

Principle #5: Live responsibly

> Let us not therefore judge one another any more: but
> judge this rather, that no man put a stumblingblock or
> an occasion to fall in his brother's way.—ROMANS 14:13

God receives us by grace, and with that grace He bestows a precious gift—Christian liberty. This is not quite the same as individual soul liberty. Soul liberty is freedom to act according to the dictates of one's conscience; Christian liberty is freedom from the bondage of sin.

A gift as valuable as Christian liberty can be gloriously enjoyed or tragically misused. Galatians 5:13 warns against its misuse: "For, brethren, ye have been called unto liberty; only use not liberty for an occasion to the flesh, but by love serve one another."

> A gift as valuable as Christian liberty can be gloriously enjoyed or tragically misused.

Yes, we have freedom from sin and liberty to set personal standards according to biblical principles and the leading of the Holy Spirit. But we dare not use our liberty to indulge in the flesh or to cause a weaker brother to stumble. To do so is to act like the irresponsible teenager bent on proving his adulthood by pushing the limits. His claim of maturity is the very evidence against his maturity!

So it is with Christians who resist personal standards and claim exemption by Christian liberty—oblivious to the effect of their actions on other Christians. Their irresponsibility is a dangerous misuse of their liberty.

God commands us to monitor our own actions for that which would cause a weaker Christian to stumble. An immature Christian leader will emphasize his liberty at the expense of his love for other believers and his loyalty to Christ. Mature Christians will accept responsibility for the effect that their actions have on younger Christians.

I like to illustrate the responsibility of leaders with the following diagram:

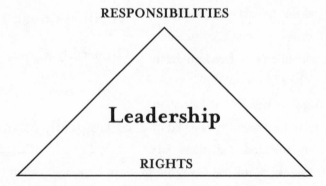

The higher you move in leadership (represented here by a triangle), the less rights you claim. Instead, you move toward responsibilities. In a sentence: leaders limit liberty.

To draw from the parallel passage in 1 Corinthians 8, Paul instructed, "But take heed lest by any means this liberty of yours become a stumbling block to them that are weak....But when ye sin so against the brethren, and wound their weak conscience, ye sin against Christ."

Did you catch that? Paul named using our liberty without consideration for others as a *sin*.

As an example, this is one of the main reasons I'm against alcohol consumption for Christian leaders. Even if I did believe Scripture permits alcohol (which I don't[10]), I wouldn't want to take the slightest chance that my liberty—expressed by wine bottles in my kitchen—would become a stumbling block to a young Christian whom I've invited to my home! Similarly, the use of many so-called "Christian songs" could likely be a stumbling block leading believers back to an ungodly lifestyle.[11] Were I to sin against brothers in Christ in this way, I'd be offending Christ Himself.

Because of my leadership position as a pastor and college president, I have felt led by the Holy Spirit to limit my liberty in various areas to be able to maintain a testimony that I believe would be pleasing to Christ. Others may feel they have liberty in areas where I have not been given freedom. This does not mean either of us is a better Christian. It means that we both must be sensitive to the Holy Spirit.

In the end, how you use your liberty really comes down to who you strive to please and for whom you assume responsibility. As a pastor, I long ago discarded the pursuit of trying to please myself in the use of liberty. And along the way, I have learned that I can't please every fundamentalist. But I have a greater concern— the growth of new Christians.

---

10 See minibook *Discerning Alcohol*, Striving Together Publications, 2005.
11 See minibook *Music Matters* by Cary Schmidt, Striving Together Publications, 2007.

In fact, my greatest concerns for how I use my Christian liberty break down as follows:

1. The Lord
2. My family
3. Local church believers
4. Other biblical Baptists

With these principles regarding liberty expressed, Paul drew a powerful conclusion: "Wherefore, if meat make my brother to offend, I will eat no flesh while the world standeth, lest I make my brother to offend" (1 Corinthians 8:13). There are some things more important than a piece of meat.

Principle #6: Be considerate

Let not then your good be evil spoken of: For the kingdom of God is not meat and drink; but righteousness, and peace, and joy in the Holy Ghost. For he that in these things serveth Christ is acceptable to God, and approved of men. Let us therefore follow after the things which make for peace, and things wherewith one may edify another.—ROMANS 14:16–19

Perhaps you've heard the phrase "perception is reality." Actually, it's not—but when it comes to something as large as the testimony of Christ, it makes little difference if someone perceives my actions as reality or if they are reality. This is why Paul cautioned, "Let not then your good be evil spoken of." In other words, don't let your use of liberty hurt Christ's testimony.

To use an old faithful fundamental Baptist illustration, I have liberty to go into a liquor store to purchase gum. But my motives may be wrongly perceived when my neighbor who is resistant to the gospel because of the hypocrisy of Christians drives by and sees me walk in.

This concern for testimony does not give me the authority to forbid church members to enter a liquor store for any purpose (although I do encourage them to distance themselves from the entire liquor industry), nor does it give me the license to judge a brother who doesn't share my view. But it does influence how I will determine standards for me and my family. And the *principle* of a godly testimony is one with which every Christian should be concerned.

Will your use of liberty damage your testimony or limit your ability to serve a particular group of believers? If so, it's better to limit yourself. This consideration for the consciences of others will ultimately expand your influence.

Principle #7: Stand in liberty

One of the wisest bits of advice I've been given in ministry came from my dear friend, Dr. Curtis Hutson. Dr. Hutson came to preach in our church when we were still in the early years of becoming established in the community. He sensed the sweet revival spirit with which God had blessed us, and over the following years, he invested himself as a mentor and encourager in my life.

When I talked to Dr. Hutson about founding West Coast Baptist College, he gave helpful insight and tremendous encouragement. But he did have one word of caution: "Don't let the presence of the college affect the spirit of the church." I asked him to illustrate what he meant, and he explained. I don't remember the exact words, but in gist, he had two concerns in mind.

The first concern was that because a college is an educational institution, it necessitates rules. In our case, the training provided is for Christian ministry, thus the rules include some enforced standards for students as well. Dr. Hutson cautioned me not to allow the regulations of institutional life seep into the personal work of local church grace-based discipleship. As a private Christian college, we can mandate a male student have a tapered haircut, but I would be remiss to insist to our church family that the biblical standard for men is the exact same.

Dr. Hutson's second concern was that we would allow the rules in the college to quench the Holy Spirit in our ministry. He warned me not to allow the pressure of trying to be non-offensive to every other church who sends students to our college to quench the liberty of simply responding to the Holy Spirit in matters of local church practice. Indeed, I do endeavor to show deference to other pastors and parents who send students to our college. But Dr. Hutson's advice has helped to keep me from being a slave to the perceptions of hundreds of churches around the country. If I believe a particular activity, song, or method would be edifying to the church which God has given me the privilege to shepherd, I stand in the liberty the Holy Spirit has given me to practice it.[12]

As independent Baptists, we resent it when Christians who have no regard for the doctrine of holiness label us *legalistic*. Our first defense is usually to point out their misuse of the word. Strictly

---

12 For more thoughts by Dr. Hutson on liberty and separation, see the booklet *Unnecessary Divisions among Fundamentalists*, Sword of the Lord Publishers, 1990. Some of the content is dated as it references concerns, but the principles are still valid.

speaking (as well as biblically speaking), *legalism* applies to adding works as a requirement to salvation.[13] *That* we vehemently abhor.

As your friend, however, allow me to use *legalistic* in a looser sense as I pass on Dr. Hutson's challenge to you. As you evaluate your liberty in Christ, live responsibly and be considerate. But don't deny your liberty. It's one thing to graciously yield to the weaker conscience of a weaker brother. It's another thing to become a slave to the dictates of every independent Baptist "camp" and their preferred standards. Paul defended those who were feeling the heat of outsiders' pressure. He instructed the Christians in Colosse, "Let no man therefore judge you in meat, or in drink, or in respect of an holyday, or of the new moon, or of the sabbath days" (Colossians 2:16).

We live in a real world where good, godly people have differences in applying biblical principles. Acknowledge this truth, seek the leading of the Holy Spirit, walk by faith, and stand in liberty.

SPLINTERED OR STRIVING?

On July 13, 1986, I stood in front of fewer than twenty people— each of us perspiring profusely in the close to one hundred degree sweltering heat of that upstairs room of our downtown church building. I had recently been voted in as the new pastor of this small, struggling congregation, and this was my first Sunday evening message as their pastor.

I chose Philippians 1:27 as my text for that evening: "Only let your conversation be as it becometh the gospel of Christ: that

---

13   Acts 15:1; Galatians 2:16–21

whether I come and see you, or else be absent, I may hear of your affairs, that ye stand fast in one spirit, with one mind striving together for the faith of the gospel."

After reading my text, I shared with the church family my vision for our church. It had nothing to do with erecting new buildings. (I was hoping we could just halfway fill the room we were in!) It had nothing to do with hiring staff. (The church couldn't pay *me* at that point.) It wasn't a vision of external grandeur.

I asked our church to be a people who would strive together for the faith of the gospel.

That was it.

And that was enough.

Almost three decades later, we're still striving together. And we're still praising God for what He will do through a people who unite around His truth and invest their energy in preaching His gospel.

If there was ever a time that Christians and local churches needed to strive together for the faith of the gospel, it is now! This is not the time for independent Baptists to divide and splinter; it is the time to reach out and turn the world upside down once again.

What could happen if each of us would participate with one another for the cause of world evangelism? What would happen if we embraced biblical separation but discarded isolation? What if we embraced propagation of the gospel but discarded polarization around personalities, institutions, or petty issues?

We're all on the same team! Instead of arguing about jersey numbers or variances in style, let's put our heart and soul into a common win.

FINAL APPLICATIONS FROM ROMANS 14

We need the spirit of unity that is fed by the Holy Spirit, committed to God's Word, and undistracted in its determination to proclaim the truth of the gospel! *This* is biblical unity—and we can't do God's work effectively without it.

Whether in the local church or among local churches, the principles of Romans 14 are vital if we are to stand in unity and strive together for the gospel. In the next few pages, I'd like to suggest a few practical admonitions from this chapter.

Respect the local church

Each pastor is accountable before God to follow biblical principle in his own life and family[14] and to teach principles to his church.[15] Hebrews 13:17 admonishes church members to respond to the pastor's leadership as a matter of principle: "Obey them that have the rule over you, and submit yourselves: for they watch for your souls, as they that must give account, that they may do it with joy, and not with grief: for that is unprofitable for you."

When I consider standing before God to give an account for the spiritual condition of those in the church I pastor, I am motivated to be faithful in watching for their souls! In that responsibility, I have established leadership requirements for our church. (In truth, every pastor has *some* leadership requirements. I don't know of any pastor who doesn't require their choir members to wear *something* as they sing for the church services!) Because I believe that every

---

14 1 Timothy 3:4–5
15 Titus 3:8

pastor has the liberty to establish leadership requirements, I will respect the leadership requirements of another church. Even if it seems to me that a pastor is too far to the right in what he asks from his leaders, I'm not going to criticize him as having a "legalistic spirit." That is between him and the Lord. Likewise, if it seems to me that he is too lax in who he allows to serve in ministry, it's not my position to judge.

Respect the Christian home

One of the greatest reasons I'm careful in how I preach on biblical principles and standards is because I desire for the men in our church to be spiritual leaders in their homes, and I'm not going to cross a father's responsibility to determine the biblical standards for his family.

Do I preach on modesty? Absolutely. And any Christian husband and father who is walking with the Lord wants his wife and daughters to be modest. But even among godly men we will have variances on what "modest" looks like. That is where Romans 14 comes in. And I will definitely defer to the God-ordained leader of the home in the specifics.

Living out the grace and liberty of Romans 14 compels us to acknowledge the authority structures God has set in our lives while allowing the Holy Spirit to work in hearts.

Don't try to be another's conscience

For most of my ministry I have battled the philosophy within independent Baptist circles of shaming or guilting people into compliance. Regrettably, in my early years of preaching, I personally tried to convince people to change without fully relying on the Holy Spirit. Then I discovered a key principle from a phrase in Hebrews 13:9, stating that our hearts are to be "established with grace." A legalistic spirit uses shame as a tool to provoke conformity; a gracious spirit inspires hope to promote transformation.

Look at this verse in its entirety: "Be not carried about with divers and strange doctrines. For it is a good thing that the heart be established with grace; not with meats, which have not profited them that have been occupied therein."

> A legalistic spirit uses shame as a tool to provoke conformity; a gracious spirit inspires hope to promote transformation.

Do you see how this fits the context of Romans 14? Making Christianity more about meat (or dress or entertainment or music or media) than grace elevates "meat" to a doctrinal position. The Christian life is to be lived by faith that is enabled by grace. Anything other than this is both inferior and dangerous.

Let people grow in grace; and leave matters of the conscience and personal change to the Holy Spirit.

Elevate Christ's testimony above your honor

We become pharisaical when we are more concerned about our honor than Christ's testimony. Our pride makes us far more prone to this than we realize, and we strive to shield our honor in ways that we realize are shameful when we step back and consider.

For instance, consider the matter of young people who grow up in fundamental churches and then leave the faith or migrate to another context of Christianity. In far too many cases, the attitude of Christian leaders toward their own children has been harsh or ostracizing. Is there not a disconnect here between the grace we preach and the gospel we live?

It is appropriate for us to feel anguish over the failures of our children but not to become hostile toward them. We may grieve their departure from the truth, but we should still love them. If our children leave their Baptist heritage, if they change their standards but love the Lord, don't fear the perception of others. Love your kids!

Those who hate your biblical position can't wait for your angry response. It gives them more opportunity to coddle and coalesce your children or members into their group identity.

Leave rules for institutions

I well understand the importance of structure and uniformity in educational institutions and with young people. But we must not allow institutional rules to become "spiritualized" and the expected behavior of church members.

Our West Coast Baptist College handbook reserves denim for ballgames and precludes facial hair on men. Frankly, the Bible does not speak to those issues. These are simply guidelines we have chosen for a variety of reasons and in the context of preparing young men and women for the ministry. Our Christian school students have a dress code for school and church, but we do not hand these guidelines to every new family or new Christian.

The Bible *does* speak of modesty, appropriateness, masculinity, and femininity. In our church, we teach and preach on these Bible principles. I do ask our ushers and choir members to wear conservative clothing; but I don't preach on whether or not men should wear jeans to church for the midweek service or if they should shave their mustache. These are institutional rules, not spiritual rules. If a member of Lancaster Baptist Church is growing in Christ and seeks to be governed by the Bible, even though he may not come to the same conclusion of application that I do in every instance, I'm thankful!

Beware of the sin of "selective standards"

As we develop personal or ministry standards based on Bible principles, our tendency is to develop a hierarchy of significance to these standards. Unlike Bible-based standards, this system is arbitrary and based on our own preferences, strengths, and weaknesses.

In fact, I've observed over the years that leaders who forcefully argue their preferences as conviction often have a weak area in their personal lives. This would be represented by the leaders who have a long and complex philosophy to their music, but they set aside issues such as Bible versions or methods of evangelism as "divisive." Or it would be represented by those who argue vehemently for the King James Bible, but they discard concerns that deal with propriety or allegations of immorality within the church.

In whatever way it is revealed, the sin of selective standards is pharisaism masquerading as fundamentalism.

Beware of pragmatism

We live in a pragmatic age. Our culture's default mentality is "if it works, it must be right" or "if I like it, I should be allowed to do it." In many cases, we've carried that logic into local church ministry and then defended it by claiming Christian liberty.

I thank God for Christian liberty. I want to give that liberty to others, and I want to receive it from them. But I also want to be discerning enough to consider how my liberty will affect the generations following me.

A spirit of pragmatism mixed with a defensive stance on liberty is like oil and fire—not only does it create a combustion, but it easily gets out of hand, running faster and further than we can control. When pastors and Christian leaders mix pragmatism with liberty, they move toward philosophies that—extrapolated out over the next decade or so—will lead to the next generation attending churches with very little semblance of doctrinal integrity or good, biblical traditions.

Younger leaders don't always have the perspective to consider the potential effect their decisions will have twenty years down the road. With that in mind, give your forefathers a vote in the decisions you make that will carry ripple effects to your descendants.

Sometimes liberty itself is promoted to such a degree that Scripture and/or thoughtful, wise discussion is discarded. Some men are not even willing to discuss issues in which they claim liberty with others in a reasonable, intellectual manner. It's as if they have become so sensitive to liberty that a brother can't even bring up an issue and prompt biblical discussion. Even as those who express their desire to use liberty don't want to be expected to embrace a standard just because someone before them chose it, they do need to be open to discussion. Liberty is vital and biblical, but if it is in charge before any issue is given a fair hearing, we push aside biblical components of wise decision-making.

The pressure of pragmatic philosophies is so heavy on pastors today that we must remember that liberty is not to be the primary criterion for decision making or for distilling biblical principles into personal standards. Liberty is key for *dealing with other brothers.* (This is the context of Romans 14.) But when it comes to making decisions—and especially decisions that are going to affect future generations—our primary sources are God's Word and His Spirit.

As my friend, Wayne Hardy, said in a recent conversation, "Liberty is to be cherished when it is used by thinking men, but it is deadly when it becomes its own virtue." In the book *Slouching Towards Gomorrah,*[16] Robert Bork makes a strong case for how the pursuit of liberty alone undermines the foundations of liberty. Unfortunately, too many American pastors are following the same trend in Christian liberty. When we pursue liberty for the sake of liberty, we miss the biblical purposes for liberty, and we cut ourselves off from both wisdom and biblical thinking.

FRIENDLY FIRE ISN'T FRIENDLY

The truths of Romans 14 regarding grace and liberty are vital to the current independent Baptist landscape. And yet, they are too frequently ignored. In these verses lie the truths that can set us free from infighting to collectively focus on the Great Commission we've been given.

---

16   Robert H. Bork, *Slouching Towards Gomorrah,* (HarperCollins, 2010).

I'm concerned that we too often have our ammunition pointed in the wrong direction.[17] Consider the spiritual battlefield in America alone: The homosexual agenda is overtaking our country. Islam is promoted, and tolerance is preached while Christians are silenced. The American government is persistently chipping away at freedom of religion and conscience. The world population is multiplying—millions perishing every day without Jesus. But while all this takes place, Baptists have their weapons aimed toward one another and are arguing about if we should sing a song that was written by someone who was not a Baptist! I'm convinced that we have veered from our mission to preach the gospel and declare the truth.

> Wanted: Christians who overlook the faults of others as easily as they do their own.

I love the quote I recently read by an unknown author, "Wanted: Christians who overlook the faults of others as easily as they do their own."

We would do well to remember the admonition of Colossians 4:6, "Let your speech be alway with grace…." We simply must stop killing one another and reposition our rifles on our real enemy—Satan.

Yes, our lives and ministries are to be distinct—holy and separated to the Lord. Yes, standards and purity are vital. But is it possible that you and I might differ on some of the specifics and still help a missionary get to the field?

---

17   For an analogy of keeping a focus on the larger issues of warfare, see Appendix 3, Instructions for American Servicemen in Britain, 1942.

When there is compromise, we must stand—without apology or wavering. But when there are godly people with slight differences, we must be gracious. That's what Romans 14 is all about.

We need a generation of spiritual leaders who will rise above petty criticism and see past minor differences. When we agree on 99.9 percent of our practices, let's encourage one another as fellow soldiers in this spiritual battle.

THE GIFT OF A GRACIOUS SPIRIT

Let's flip the coin for a minute. Just as vital as it is for preachers to encourage one another, giving grace while keeping doctrinal integrity, so it is important for those on the receiving end to respond in grace—especially toward those who have been their mentors in the faith.

While there is room for difference, growth, and discovery, and while not every leader is going to land on the same personal beliefs, I have noticed an attitude that places a young leader on a "slippery slope." In fact, it's not the early changes he may make so much as it is his attitude in those changes. The clearest indicator of a real heart problem in change that I see is when a young leader uses his Christian liberty to flaunt his flesh and to rub it in the face of his earlier mentors.

Too many young leaders miss the underlying heart for God and passion for purity of the older generation. Instead of honoring and respecting those who have invested into their lives and labored to preserve truth, they snatch up new areas of liberty and turn back to the older generation with sneering accusations of "legalists" and "traditionalists."

If you are a young leader, I'd like to encourage you to buck that trend. Rather than using your liberty spitefully, employ it lovingly and gratefully.

I myself differ in some minor points from godly men who have mentored me. (For instance, Lee Roberson was *insistent* that I should require our choir to wear robes!) I'm thankful, however, that as a young man, I had enough wisdom to choose to respect and honor mentors with whom I had slight differences. I never did ask our choir to wear robes, but neither did I preach against the "legalism" of Dr. Roberson for believing it was important. Looking back over the years, I am grateful beyond measure for the influence men of Dr. Roberson's generation had in my life. To shed it all because I felt they were harsh or outdated would have been a costly mistake for me.

> When we agree on 99.9 percent of our practices, let's encourage one another as fellow soldiers in this spiritual battle.

No one is perfect. Please have the grace to give your mentors and leaders room to be human—to have blind spots they may never even realize. Even those who deeply disappointed me had some lessons that were biblical and useful. We must not be too quick to react against everything taught to us by men who were different in application or even those who failed in application of Scripture. The graciousness to be grateful to those who have helped us is a sure mark of our own growth in grace.

FINDING BALANCE AND GIVING GRACE

As preachers of God's Word, we are committed to declaring truth and exposing error. For the glory of God and the sake of those to whom we minister, we are compelled to make a clear line of demarcation between right and wrong. We see issues in black and white, and we call them for what they are.

But what if all of life is not displayed in black and white? What if there are some areas in which God gives us the liberty to paint with the vibrant colors He created? Could we be mistaken in calling something black that is really a dark hue of purple?

Not too long ago, I preached at two conferences, conducted just a few weeks apart, in different parts of the country. Both conferences were conducted by dear friends in the ministry.

The music at these two meetings differed from each other, and they were both different than the music style at Lancaster Baptist Church. In one church, the music was extremely conservative. A few of the songs were much more formal than I am accustomed to. Their large string orchestra played with the congregational hymns. All in all, it set a backdrop for rich worship and exalting Christ. At one point during the conference, they opened the floor to prayer. Men from across the auditorium spontaneously lifted their voices in prayer for God's power in the meeting, for conviction and renewal in their lives, and for revival in the nation. It was orderly, spontaneous, and refreshing. I loved it!

A few weeks later, I preached at a conference in which the music was—within the realms of conservative music—the polar opposite of the first conference. They had three acoustic guitars on the platform and down home style gospel music. The congregation was more vocally responsive to the special music ("Amen!! Preach it,

Brother!"). The music in these two churches was different in every respect. But the second conference likewise had a time of prayer. Here, they began the meeting by asking the men to come forward and spend time in prayer. Immediately, men responded. From the front of the church they lifted their voices in prayer. They asked God for His power; they asked Him to reveal sin in their lives and to help them walk closely with Him; they asked for revival in their churches and across our nation. Wait…they were praying for the exact requests as the men at the first meeting!

Was one style of music right and the other wrong? I'll leave that as a matter between those two pastors and the Holy Spirit. For my part, I was blessed and enriched by the worship and fellowship in *both* meetings. I don't believe the music at either place—all of which was rendered with hearts dedicated to God—was black or white. I think it was all vibrant shades of color expressing Christians' pure hearts of worship to the Lord.

More concerning to me than variance in styles of godly music is when good, fundamental, revival-longing people have a spirit of condemnation for one another. No Christian is perfectly balanced in his standards—no leader, no critic, no friend—nobody. Truthfully, biblical balance is a journey, and experience is gained along the trail.

I wonder how God may bless our road ahead if instead of despising one another, we consistently gave Romans 14 grace?

Engage Younger Pastors in Ministry Conversation

THE OTHER DAY MY THREE-YEAR-OLD grandson and I were having lunch together—spending Papa and Camden time, just the two of us. We talked about the usual things—playing ball in the yard, his rabbits, the projects he and his mom or dad had worked on together, and his soon-to-be-born little brother.

Suddenly, Camden paused mid-sentence. I couldn't imagine what he might say next, but by the intent look on his face, I could see his wheels were turning.

I watched, beaming with pride at my near-genius grandson. Camden stared at me for several seconds, and I wondered what profound truth he was assimilating.

"Papa," he said, "you don't got any hair on top!"

My smile faded. "Why, no, I guess I don't....Hey, Buddy, what do you say we go play ball in the living room?"

"But, Papa, *why* you have no hair on top?" Camden is not so easily distracted. Before the conversation turned, he felt the top of his head and pointed out that he had hair on the top *and* the sides of his head while I only had hair on the sides. His observations were correct, but that fact didn't make me eager to prolong our conversation!

There's nothing like the questions of a three-year-old to keep a conversation real. And there's nothing like the perception of a child to keep adults authentic!

Honest questions and transparent answers are vital marks of authenticity—especially when it comes to the ministry.

The openness and sincerity of those younger than us sometimes makes an older preacher feel uncomfortably vulnerable; yet it is important that we do not discourage someone from conversation simply because they are young, honest, and inquisitive. As younger preachers engage in the ministry, they bring a set of fresh questions and sometimes painfully valid concerns. There is an authenticity and blunt honesty in their observations.

It's not uncommon for me to receive an email from a younger pastor with a subject line something like "A few questions" or "Concerns re: affiliations." Usually, the message that follows expresses confusion or struggles regarding sin, inconsistency, or troubling personalities among other independent Baptist churches.

Since the coinage of the term "IFB" (which I had never heard as initials only for an identifying moniker prior to the media's and critics' use of it a couple of years ago), it is more concerning than ever to these younger men to be "lumped in" with leaders and pastors over whom they have no control or influence. Their questions range from frustrated to penetrating. Often, they are looking toward the future and calculating the pros and cons of continuing to identify themselves and their churches with their heritage, affiliations, and associations.

Historically, when there have been sins and inconsistencies in the leadership of any Christian movement, the younger men within particular groups responded by switching movements or groups because of their discouragement or disillusionment.

In some instances, this may be exactly what the Holy Spirit directed them to do. If the move is toward pure doctrine and a godly lifestyle, certainly this would be the case. Many leaders of the past—Curtis Hutson, Lee Roberson, and B. Myron Cedarholm, for example—did not start in ministry as independent Baptists. Each of these men saw the corrupted doctrine and deterioration of godliness within mainstream conventions and pulled out. We thank God for their courage.

> Honest questions and transparent answers are vital marks of authenticity— especially when it comes to ministry.

On the other hand, because of the underlying discouragement or disillusionment in play, there is always the danger of overreaction. It's all too easy to throw out the baby with the bath water. I've seen good young leaders, failing to differentiate the foolish practices of an early mentor from some of his biblical positions in truth, throw out everything they associate with him. Frustrated at his sin, they ditch everything the mentor taught or preached.

When a leader or a movement reaches a crossroads of identification and heritage, it is vital that we make a distinction between extra-biblical preferences and biblical position. While we may look for new nomenclature or verbiage with which to describe ourselves, we must never abandon our historical, doctrinal position.

So, how do you answer the legitimate concerns of a young leader who is considering switching groups or struggling with difficult identities? In this chapter, I would like to share some important principles for seasoned pastors as they talk to young pastors who are working through these issues in their own minds.

If you are a young pastor or spiritual leader, please read thoughtfully. I respect you, and I thank God for your willingness to serve Him in the gospel ministry and to read this book.

If you are an "older" (define this word for yourself) leader—perhaps sometimes perturbed by the questions of the younger generation—I pray these thoughts will be a help to you as well. It's not wrong for younger men to have questions. Questions are healthy and good—and they prove a man is thinking. But, it *is* wrong for us to respond to their questions with a spirit of pride, wondering why they would dare question our practices. Some younger pastors feel they cannot ask sincere questions or pose genuine dialogue lest their intentions be misunderstood.

Remember, we Baptists believe in the autonomy of the local church. This necessitates that every pastor—regardless of his age or his alma mater—be fully settled in his own spirit that what he preaches and practices is biblical and that he is following the headship of Christ.

Just prior to this writing, I invited twenty younger pastors to an informal day-long meeting in which we covered several present-day challenges in ministry. Additionally, we had some helpful "round table" discussion giving these men the opportunity to dialogue concerning their questions.

When those of us who have pastored for many years are solidly grounded in our position, questions are not a threat; they are a chance to explain the legitimacy of what we believe and practice.

So, with that in mind, allow me to share a pattern for your interaction with tomorrow's biblical Baptist leaders.

Listen intently

Proverbs 18:13 cautions, "He that answereth a matter before he heareth it, it is folly and shame unto him." And James 1:19 adds, "let every man be swift to hear, slow to speak, slow to wrath." So I listen intently.

I learn a lot about someone's spirit by his tone of voice (which is one reason I don't care much for lengthy email communication). If I don't listen first, I can't hear the tone.

Do they have a legitimate frustration? Is their concern regarding a particular group within independent Baptists, or is it regarding the foundational principles of our movement? Are they being courted by another group who hopes to add a name to their published statistics of church planters?

Not every question has the same thought process backing it, and some questions may be a lead-in to deeper, more heart-specific questions. Sometimes a young pastor's heart is shifting. Sometimes he is simply growing and needs someone to listen while he sorts it all out. If I dismiss him with a pat answer, I may end the discussion with a victory mark on my mental scoreboard. But ultimately, it's a loss to me. I don't *want* to end the discussion. I want to hear him think, and I want to be involved in his process of coming to a Bible-based conclusion.

I have another, perhaps selfish, reason for listening intently to younger pastors: I glean fresh ideas from them. They are a gold mine of bright, new ideas. Younger men have a unique perspective. If I quenched every idea by men who are in their twenties or thirties ("Oh, they'll mature in time" or "My granddad didn't do it that way"), I'd be missing out on an abundance of good ideas.

Listen to young pastors. Take them seriously. Some of the leaders I greatly respect are young men with a fervent love for God and a passion to reach the lost.

Talk kindly

Unless you are a cookie-cutter pastor (and for the sake of those in your ministry, I hope you're not!), you went through your own process of discovering and defining ministry philosophy. Perhaps your process was internal. Perhaps you developed yours in Bible college. Perhaps you readily adapted to the philosophies of your mentors. But whatever the case, you do have a ministry philosophy, and you developed it over a period of time.

When I became a pastor, I was grounded in doctrine, but I did discover many aspects of ministry that I had not previously understood. I'm thankful for older pastors who didn't write me off because I asked questions (and looking back, I see that I asked a *lot* of questions) or tried a new method (many of which I fortunately had the sense to never repeat).

Let's give today's young leaders the room to also develop their ministry philosophy. Let's not be too quick to criticize a method that is different from ours or happens to have been borrowed from another group. The truth is, other groups *do* sometimes utilize one or more biblical methods, and *new* doesn't always mean *wrong*.

Ecclesiastes 10:12 describes the kind wisdom of many of my early mentors who watched me grow: "The words of a wise man's mouth are gracious." I want to extend that gracious spirit to the leaders growing around me.

Talk patiently

To listen to the talking heads on the Internet, you'd gather that young guys are leaving fundamentalism *en masse*, that biblical Baptists are on the brink of extinction! Apparently, the critics have some insight I don't, because I believe that independent Baptist churches have some of the largest percentage of young men in Bible colleges of any group I know. In fact, the vast majority of the men I talk to are thankful for their heritage and grounded in their doctrine.

Don't let the pressure of fear drive you into crisis mode when a young pastor approaches you with a question regarding his heritage. Be patient. Give him space to reason through his concerns without forcing him to an artificial crossroads.

Despite the predictions of critics, most of these young men will remain Baptist, grow in grace, and appreciate the good influence in their lives. In fact, some will become *more* secure in biblical, conservative ministry by having taken the time to seriously think through the various issues. Be patient.

Talk biblically

The young guys I talk to are pretty passionate to say, "Show me that in Scripture." While it might be unnerving if you really don't know where your ministry philosophy is found in Scripture, their quest for straight Bible truth is admirable! Don't take it as a personal affront or a distrust of your character. Encourage it.

The Bible speaks directly on all the main issues. And, because I'm confident that the aspects of ministry which I believe to be vital are directly addressed in Scripture, I don't mind someone asking for a chapter and verse. I am glad to open my Bible and discuss it. If you are familiar with God's Word and your ministry is firmly tied to its principles, it's not difficult to "speak...the things which become sound doctrine" (Titus 2:1).

At the same time, I recognize that I do have preferences in ministry. For example, I wear a tie for Wednesday night Bible study. But I would be silly to insist this is a biblical doctrine or to write off a young pastor because he does not wear a tie on Wednesday evenings. I have found most pastors appreciate it when I freely admit if something is a personal preference. It lends credibility to your convictions when you acknowledge your preferences.

Talk reasonably

Who doesn't appreciate honesty? I have found it is easier to discuss the weaknesses of other groups when we admit the weaknesses of our own circles.

For example, I see some of the following weaknesses on both sides of the fence:

Weaknesses of Some Fundamental Baptists	Weaknesses of Some Non-Denominationalists
Lack of discipleship	Lack of soulwinning
Strange people get headlines (it's uncomfortable and disturbing to be strapped to an unfair caricature of your beliefs)	Strange people get headlines
Glory in standards	Belittle the doctrine of holiness, endorse alcohol consumption, glory in fleshly liberty
Personal beliefs lifted to level of Bible doctrine	Angry, promotion of hyper-Calvinism, non-cessationist
Critical spirit toward other believers	Critical spirit toward fundamentalists

Every group has weaknesses because all groups are comprised of humans. It's only reasonable to acknowledge the inconsistencies within our own movement.

By the same token, it's okay to admit that a group to your "left" may have a strength. For example, I'm thankful for any preacher who preaches against abortion or teaches the blood atonement.

An honest, reasonable look at the strengths and weaknesses of various groups helps younger men realize that the green grass on the other side of the fence has as many brown patches as the grass under their own feet. Considering that every group has its flaws, I remind young men that the answer isn't normally found by changing groups, but by asking God to change "me."

Talk lovingly

It often seems a little-known truth, but when the Bible instructs us in Christian charity, it never gives an exception clause for those who don't believe exactly the same as we do! Because of this, and because I really do thank God for every man who is preaching the gospel, I've decided to go on loving younger pastors who do not practice my preferences or even my convictions in certain areas.

> It lends credibility to your convictions when you acknowledge your preferences.

I may not have a peace to invite them to preach in our ministry, but if I'm in their city, I'd like to have a meal with them and hear what God is doing in their lives. And I surely want to know when they are in a personal time of need so I can pray for, visit, or otherwise encourage them.

I have a younger pastor friend whose ministry philosophy is not what I practice, but we are kind toward one another. He prayed for my son during his battle with cancer, and I am praying now for his daughter with leukemia.

Based on Ephesians 6:24, it seems the Apostle Paul took a similar stance: "Grace be with all them that love our Lord Jesus Christ in sincerity. Amen." If Paul, on the other hand, positioned himself like many twenty-first-century independent Baptists, he might have said, "Grace be with all them who adhere to my preferences and espouse my exact ministry philosophy."

Talk securely

Some men are like a plane circling in a holding pattern before landing—they may circle the issues over and over before they really settle. But, after thirty-three years of preaching, I am no longer circling—I have already landed on the main issues. I don't feel threatened to discuss them, nor am I concerned that an article I read may sway my stance.

Young men today need to know that this kind of security in position is not only possible, but desirable. In the epistles Paul sent to Timothy and Titus, four times he said, "This is a faithful saying…" and then referred to doctrinal truth (1 Timothy 1:15, 4:9; 2 Timothy 2:11; Titus 3:8). Timothy and Titus had no doubt as to Paul's security in his beliefs.

Talk assuredly

Beyond the core doctrines of the faith, there are four truths I am assured of. Each of these has significant bearing on my willingness to dialogue with young preachers who are questioning.

First, if a spiritual leader maintains a sensitivity to the Holy Spirit, a tender heart, and is not hurt by or angry at an authority figure, he will not react to issues by moving to an extreme position.

Second, if a pastor has been thoroughly grounded and settled in the faith, he normally will not depart from orthodoxy. (Incidentally, a man who says he was not properly grounded in Bible college must realize that it may not have been the fault of the college.)

Third, every group has its weaknesses and failures. Men who get angry at the problems in one group and react by moving to another group will inevitably find a new set of weaknesses.

Fourth, God is sovereign, and His work will be done by many or few.[1] Contrary to current thought, He doesn't need a network, a fellowship, or a denomination. He uses sanctified vessels who want to give Him the glory.

Talk hopefully

Who wants to be part of a dying remnant?! Young pastors want to be with men who are *for* something and who have optimism for tomorrow.

Paul seemed to know this, and he remembered it as he reported to his sending church after his first missionary journey. He had just traveled some fourteen hundred miles through physically challenging territory, preached the gospel throughout Asia minor, been deserted by a member of his traveling party, been repeatedly beset by unbelieving Jews, and been stoned and left for dead—all in the space of approximately two years. Yet, when he gave the report of his trip, he emphasized the positive aspects of God's work and pointed to the souls being saved: "And when they were come, and had gathered the church together, they rehearsed all that God had done with them, and how he had opened the door of faith unto the Gentiles" (Acts 14:27).

When I talk to young men, I like to talk about people recently saved and the new families added to our church who have recently been reached through personal soulwinning. I talk about growing

---

1   1 Samuel 14:6

numbers of missionaries being sent out from likeminded churches. I talk about the positive qualities of growing churches around the world.

I talk about the men of the previous generation who ministered faithfully—faithful to the Word, their spouse, and the Lord. Some younger men haven't heard much about these men, so I share a few details:

Fred Donnelson (1897–1974)—Fred was one of the men who pulled out of a liberal convention, leading his church to become an independent Baptist church. He and his wife Effie spent several years as missionaries in China before he became the first missions director for the Baptist Bible Fellowship (BBF). His passion to reach the world with the gospel was so intense that he led scores of others to a life of missions.

Bob Hughes (1932–1977)—Bob and Helen Hughes served in the Philippines as missionaries for twenty years where they planted the Bible Baptist Church in Cebu City. Through ministry in the Philippines, Bob led thousands to Christ before he was diagnosed with cancer and was forced to return to the United States for treatment. In spite of the fast-advancing cancer, Bob used the remaining eleven months of his life to encourage independent Baptists to see the vast need of world evangelism. Missionary Rick Martin surrendered to serve in the Philippines while listening to Bob Hughes in the final weeks of his life.

B. R. Lakin (1901–1984)—As a teenager, B. R. Lakin served as a circuit riding preacher for churches near the backwoods areas of West Virginia and Kentucky where he was raised, riding a mule from church to church. Later, as a pastor and then finally as an evangelist,

Dr. Lakin is said to have seen 100,000 conversions through his ministry. Over 5,000 people attended his memorial service.

B. Myron Cedarholm (1915–1997)—Dr. Cedarholm was one of the men who watched the Northern Baptist Convention decline, attempted to turn the tide, and finally pulled out of the convention. Because of his firm convictions regarding biblical authority and preaching and his concern that younger men be trained in biblical ministry, Dr. Cedarholm founded Maranatha Baptist Bible College. Those who were privileged to be trained under his ministry remember his insistence that God's Word be central in preaching. He had a particular passion for church planting and evangelism.

Lee Roberson (1909–2007)—After a few comparatively brief pastorates, Dr. Roberson became the pastor of the Highland Park Baptist Church in Chattanooga, Tennessee. Almost 65,000 people were added to Highland Park in the forty years Dr. Roberson was the pastor. Almost 40,000 of these were added through believer's baptism. In many ways, Dr. Roberson was an innovative pioneer in independent Baptist circles. He founded Tennessee Temple University and Seminary, both of which trained thousands of Christian servants. Highland Park began a citywide bus ministry and founded Camp Joy. He greatly influenced fundamentalism and independent Baptists with his preaching ministry which continued until he went to Heaven at the age of ninety-seven. I particularly appreciated Dr. Roberson's willingness to mentor me and his focus on compassionate soulwinning and being filled with the Holy Spirit.

Tom Malone (1915–2007)—Nineteen-year-old Tom Malone was saved at a Methodist church. At Bob Jones University he learned about soulwinning—and his life was completely transformed.

From the moment he led that first soul to Christ, he never lost his heart for personal evangelism. For over fifty years, he pastored the Emmanuel Baptist Church in Pontiac, Michigan, which was one of the largest churches in America for some time. A good ol' farm boy, Dr. Malone never lost his down-to-earth personality and approachability. He remained firm in a strong fundamental stand, but he maintained a gracious spirit that will always be a credit to fundamentalism. Dr. Malone was highly educated, yet his humble and gracious spirit toward me and our church left an indelible impression.

Curtis Hutson (1934–1995)—Curtis Hutson was a bi-vocational pastor of a struggling church when he first heard teaching on personal soulwinning. Less than one week later, after having led three people to Christ, Curtis Hutson was hooked for life. In 1977, Dr. Hutson entered full-time evangelism, and a year later he joined John R. Rice as the associate editor for *The Sword of the Lord*. Upon Dr. Rice's death two years later, Dr. Hutson became the editor of the *Sword*. He led thousands of people to Christ before he died of cancer in 1995.

Don Sisk (1933–)—The first time I met Dr. Sisk was at a rather peculiar pastors' conference. A young pastor (still in my twenties), I was appalled at the blatancy with which preferences were being forcefully preached as truth and with the weird loyalty some men expressed to a dominant leader at the meeting. Dr. Sisk's genuinely joyful spirit and his kind interest in me did more to steady my spirit than he could have known at the time. Since then, he has become my strongest mentor in the ministry. Don and Virginia Sisk traveled to Japan in 1965 where they planted two indigenous churches (one of which is the largest Baptist church in Japan to this day) and established the Kansai Independent Baptist Bible School. Later, Dr. Sisk served for almost two decades as the President and General Director of Baptist International Missions Incorporated (BIMI). When he "retired" from BIMI, Dr. Sisk agreed to serve as the Chairman of the Missions Department for West Coast Baptist College—a decision for which I will forever be grateful. I believe he has done more to influence young people for missions than anyone in this generation. Only eternity will reveal the impact of his life.

Rick Martin (1952–)—You won't meet a man more dedicated to Christ and loving to people than Rick Martin. For over thirty-five years, Rick and his wife Becky have served in the Philippines. The Martins planted Iloilo Baptist Church in the downstairs garage of an apartment building. Today, the church occupies a five thousand seat auditorium. When I visited last year, the back doors of their *overflow* room were opened, and the crowd was spilling out into the street and beyond. Through the Bible college Dr. Martin founded, Filipino workers have established over one thousand churches throughout the Philippines—and this number doesn't even take into account the churches planted by missionaries these churches have sent to other countries. I know of no greater missionary work being done in the world today.

Each of the men above has had different strengths (and, yes, weaknesses too), but all of them—and thousands more—have been used by God as willing vessels. In every group, there will be divisive personalities, talking heads, and weird leaders; but I want young pastors to know that independent Baptists have—and have had—holy, godly men who live to please God and lead people to Christ.

Talk heavenly

Ultimately, my greatest contribution to younger pastors will not be conveyed through personal conversations, but through heavenly conversations. The greatest investment I can make in younger generations is that of fervent prayer.

I pray for myself to be the right example and to remain faithful. I pray for these pastors to reach their generation with the gospel. I pray for them to keep an eternal perspective and to live and serve for an audience of One.[2]

LOOKING UNTO JESUS

As Christian leaders, we engage in the front lines of spiritual warfare. In any war, it is too easy to focus on present skirmishes and lose sight of the larger picture. While we squabble over personality differences, our nation is becoming less tolerant of Christianity. While we focus on "issues" and wrestle over inside loyalties, souls are perishing into *eternity*—this is not a cliché; it is reality. Can we really afford to live in the flesh while we fight a spiritual battle?

We need leaders today—young and old—who will walk uprightly, win souls, and build churches. We need young men who disentangle themselves from concerns about the eccentric people who identify themselves as independent Baptists as well as from the popular momentum of church growth experts. We need young pastors who will study God's Word and follow biblical principles

---

2   For more thoughts concerning the unique challenges and victories for older and younger preachers, see Appendix 4 with the article "Concerns and Hopes for Preachers."

by personal conviction—but more than that, by love-based loyalty to Jesus Christ.

We desperately need a revival of biblically centered, Holy Spirit-sent momentum in our midst once again. That sort of a revival will only come as we refocus our eyes away from the conflicting views of other leaders and look unto Jesus, the author and finisher of our faith.

Return to
Soulwinning and Outreach

To SAY THAT OUR NATION is speeding down a slippery slope is not an understatement. It would be more accurate to say that we are careening toward a frightening cliff. Morally, politically, financially, socially, and spiritually, we long ago untied our beliefs and practices from our early faith and values. Short of the intervention of revival, the future is deeply concerning.

Ours is a time period of internal corruption and hostility toward Christians. But it's been like this before. I am reminded of a time more dire than ours—the days in which John the Baptist began preaching. By Roman authority, Herod Antipas governed Judea and Samaria with pettiness and self-interest. The ruling Jewish leaders treated John the Baptist with contempt. Yet he was faithful to his calling to "prepare the way of the Lord."

Our responsibility today is similar to John the Baptist's. We, too, are preparing for the coming of our Lord. "For if we believe that Jesus died and rose again, even so them also which sleep in Jesus will God bring with him" (1 Thessalonians 4:14).

I look forward to Christ's return with eager anticipation. But until then, I long to make a difference in this generation—to prepare the way of the Lord.

If we will make a difference in this generation, we must return to the biblical priorities of our spiritual forefathers. In this chapter, I want to encourage Baptist leaders to return to these priorities with great fervor.

PERSONALLY ENGAGE IN SOULWINNING

The mission of every local church is "Go ye into all the world, and preach the gospel to every creature" (Mark 16:15; see also Matthew 28:18–20 and Acts 1:8). But to break it down further, the personal order to every Christian is to be "ambassadors for Christ, as though God did beseech you by us"; our job is to stand "in Christ's stead" imploring sinners, "be ye reconciled to God" (2 Corinthians 5:20).

To obey our personal orders we must personally be soul conscious. If we depend on conferences or latest strategies to keep us engaged in personal evangelism, we'll be sporadic in our efforts at best. But if we discipline ourselves in prayer and action to focus on our mission, we'll see every person with whom we interact as an individual with an eternal soul. We'll make and schedule time for purposed soulwinning, and we'll be responsive to the Holy Spirit's promptings to witness as we go about our regular business. Should we not return to an overwhelming focus of obeying the explicit orders of Christ?

Not too long ago, a pastor whom I did not know called to ask for some advice. He introduced himself and told me he was struggling to balance his life—especially between family and ministry. I asked him a few questions about his family and his church so I could understand what he was up against. As it turned out, he pastored a small church in a promising town. The church was able to support him and his family, but he wanted to see the church grow, and he was sure the Lord did as well. But he didn't want to lose his family in the process.

> I long to make a difference in this generation—to prepare the way of the Lord.

"So tell me," I questioned, "how long has it been since you had a family night?"

"A few weeks." I could hear the reluctance to answer in his voice. "Well, actually, a few months."

I'm sympathetic to the struggle to balance the ministry and family—it's a common concern for every pastor I know. I figured this pastor must have just let family time slip while he was overly consumed with the church.

"When do you normally go out soulwinning?" I questioned.

Silence. "Umm, well, I haven't gone out soulwinning for several weeks. You see, I'm really struggling to balance my priorities."

Wow! I didn't know where to start. How do you help someone balance what they don't do?

We Baptists *say* leading people to Christ is the highest priority of a Christian. But do we make any effort to do it? Or do we let our schedules fill and our intentions fade so that our time fritters away with nothing of eternal consequence to show for it?

We used to criticize "armchair professors" for arguing about the finer points of theology while failing to personally reach people with the gospel. But we are sometimes guilty of the same crime— only our discussions have stooped lower! Rather than debating theological issues, we comment and blog about personality and practice issues. Meanwhile, people die without salvation and go to a Christless Hell.

What would it take for you to disengage from the superficial world of talk and passionately pour your focus into obeying Christ's Great Commission?

Like Jesus, a spiritual leader with an eternal focus will sense urgency and say, "I must work the works of him that sent me, while it is still day: the night cometh, when no man can work" (John 9:4).

LEAD YOUR CHURCH IN BIBLICAL PRIORITIES

Being a faithful soulwinner and building a soulwinning church only happens by intention. It must be purposeful, and it must be a priority.

From the early days of the independent Baptist movement, this focus on personal soulwinning and evangelism was, like missions, one of our greatest strengths. As pastors of independent Baptist churches went from house to house with the gospel and taught their members to do the same, churches swelled and flourished with young Christians.[1] The booming independent Baptist growth of the 1970s and 80s wasn't a random phenomenon. It was the result of personal, passionate, and compassionate soulwinning.

What would it take for you to commit to lead your church to become more fervent in its soulwinning efforts?

Here are a few practical suggestions:

1. Lead by example. Soulwinning is better caught than taught. People do what people see, so model soulwinning yourself by being faithful. Plan quality gatherings for evangelism on a weekly basis, and be sure to attend these gatherings and to lead in the outreach efforts.

2. Train faithful men. The most valuable gift you can give another person is a good example with personal mentoring. I encourage the trained soulwinners in our church to find and train a new partner every several months. In this way, more Christians are personally invited to begin soulwinning, and at the same time, they are given hands-on training.

3. Motivate soulwinners. Encourage your church family to develop and maintain a heart for soulwinning by having soulwinning testimonies shared in church, writing personal notes of encouragement to those who are communicating their faith, and preaching on the eternal priorities of the gospel.

4. Provide multiple soulwinning opportunities. You don't have to be a large church to be an effective soulwinning church. But you do need some organization. Schedule times throughout the week when church members can pair up at church with another

---

1   See the book *To Seek and to Save* for a comprehensive approach to soulwinning training for the local church. Sword of the Lord Publishers, 1998.

soulwinner to systematically bring the gospel to every home in your community. At these meetings, share Scripture and have prayer.

Besides different scheduled times, I recommend different types of calls as well. Some people may go door to door, while others visit "new move ins" to the community, and others may follow up on last Sunday's visitors.

5. Be diligent in tracking contacts. For many years I have maintained an active soulwinning prospect list, and I have taught our church family to do the same. On my list I collect names and addresses of people I have met or visited who have shown an interest in visiting church or in hearing the gospel. I strive to call, visit, or write every person on my prospect list at least once a week. Scores of the people in our church today were once on my or another soulwinner's prospect list. I've seen the Lord bless this diligence over and over again.

DISCIPLE NEW CONVERTS

If the zeal for soulwinning and missions within independent Baptists has had a weak link, it is in this area of mentoring and discipling new converts.

As a preacher's son growing up in the 1970s I had the privilege of being around great preachers. I thrilled to hear of the "big days" across the nation when buses would overflow and church attendance would swell. But as I grew a little older, I wondered, *Where were all the people that came on the Big Day?* As I began to formulate a ministry philosophy as a young pastor, I determined to nurture young Christians to grow in the Lord.

From our earliest days in Lancaster, Terrie and I have often invited new Christians (who made up the majority of our church membership in those years) to our home. We'd teach them the basics of Bible doctrine, and we'd encourage them to take steps of obedience in their Christian life. We'd take them soulwinning with us and invite them to work alongside us at church work days so we could mentor and influence them. We'd have new member classes in our home and teach young Christians to establish a personal walk with God.

As our church grew and some of these younger Christians matured, we were able to share the discipleship responsibilities with others. We wrote out a discipleship curriculum and formalized it into part of our church's weekly schedule.[2]

Each Wednesday night at Lancaster Baptist, disciplers from adult Bible classes meet with their assigned new Christians and work through our *Daily in the Word* discipleship material. Those Christians who complete their courses have a smaller attrition rate, a better understanding of Scriptures, and they have formed healthy friendships in the process.

I believe that high attendance weekends of ministry must not be viewed as a benchmark accomplishment to record and pass forward, but as a starting point for continued discipleship and training. Aggressive soulwinning must be followed with aggressive discipleship.

Jesus told His disciples that by bearing "much fruit" they would glorify the Father (John 15:8). But in the same conversation, His repeated instructions described the fruit He wanted them to

---

2   See Striving Together Publications (strivingtogether.com) for discipleship materials.

bear: "Ye have not chosen me, but I have chosen you, and ordained you, that ye should go and bring forth fruit, and that your *fruit should remain...*" (John 15:16).

If we are to see renewal among our churches and across our nation, we must return to regular soulwinning and passionate discipleship.

REACH EVERY CULTURAL GROUP

Everyone in this country, no matter how they got here or when and where they came from, is in need of Christ. It is not only a missions opportunity, but it is our responsibility to reach every cultural group in our community. With Hispanic communities growing throughout our country, few churches have reason not to begin a Spanish ministry.

One of my great joys is seeing the growth of a large congregation of Spanish-speaking people who gather on our campus every week. Just this past Tuesday evening, I greeted our Spanish soulwinning class. Over one hundred people were learning how to win souls and preparing to witness for Christ that very evening.

ESTABLISH CAMPUS MINISTRIES

Much of the change in modern America began twenty-five years ago in public school curricula and programs. Children have been desensitized to biblical teaching through programs like "anti-bullying" that would often be better described as "back down" propaganda for the gay agenda.[3] These tender hearts and pliable minds are being influenced against God before their consciences are even fully developed. If there is a group that we must reach with the gospel, it is the children in American public schools.

Bus ministries can and do reach children, but there are many more who will never ride our buses. Because the law allows for clubs, including Christian clubs on high school campuses, we have worked with local Christian teachers to establish Bible clubs on several high school campuses. The impact has been eternal!

Another often overlooked "mission field" is the campuses of secular universities. Here the anti-God movement has had its foothold for decades. Students in these universities are inundated with philosophy that not only denies God, but fiercely opposes Him and resists any standards of morality.

> Aggressive soulwinning must be followed with aggressive discipleship.

We can see the young adults of these universities as being an annoyance and perhaps a threat to the future of our nation as they integrate intolerant philosophies. Or, we can see them as a tremendous mission field.

There may be no life stage that faces stronger spiritual warfare than that of single adults. Satan wants to rule this time of life, yet God's more abundant life must be shared with this generation with joy and energy. A recent study showed that religious "nones,"

---

3   "Anti-Bullying Campaign Demeans Christians," May 1, 2012, http://www. paulchappell.com/2012/05/01/anti-bullying-campaign-demeans-christians/.

those who identified with no religion, has risen to 20 percent of Americans. Among adults ages 18–22, the proportion is 34 percent.[4]

In the recent presidential election, the Democratic Party ran buses from these campuses to polling places. Perhaps we could follow their lead and run buses from the campuses to Bible-preaching churches. We can also establish Bible clubs on these campuses. As local churches, we must not take the attitude that, "Someone else will reach our Jerusalem." It is our responsibility, and we must not abandon the spiritual destiny of the next generation to parachurch organizations.

PLANT CHURCHES

When it comes to planting churches, I think we romanticize the spiritual condition of our nation. For instance, within a 350-mile radius of Lancaster, there are well over ten million people (and that's a conservative estimate)—mostly in cities with few or no gospel preaching churches:

Los Angeles: 3.8 million

San Diego: 1.3 million

San Jose: 1 million

San Francisco: 805,000

Fresno: 500,000

Long Beach: 500,000

Las Vegas, Nevada: 500,000

Many Christians believe that we already have an adequate number of churches in the United States and that we need to focus our

---

4   "'Nones' on the Rise," Pew Research Center, October 9, 2012, http://www. pewforum.org/Unaffiliated/nones-on-the-rise.aspx.

church-planting efforts elsewhere. The truth, however, is that America is rapidly becoming a mission field. [5]

In particular, the inner cities of America have largely been abandoned by Bible-preaching churches, but the souls of people in these areas matter to God. Lancaster Baptist has started the Victory Baptist Church in North Hollywood-Burbank and the Los Angeles Baptist Church, but we need a hundred more in these densely populated areas.[6] We need far fewer discussions and much greater action.

It is the local church that has been commissioned by Christ to declare the gospel. Thus, we must be planting more churches. Remember, we need not wait for a denomination or fellowship to start new churches. Churches start churches (Acts 13:1), and it's time to get our churches involved in the process. Pray for specific areas that need a gospel-preaching church, and ask God to send forth laborers for that area.

ENLARGE YOUR HEART FOR WORLD MISSIONS

I'll never forget the piercing question our guide at the Temple of Heaven in China asked several years ago. She spoke some English, and I carefully explained the gospel to her. She listened intently as I spoke of Christ's death, burial, and resurrection and then described His free offer of salvation. I was surprised by her question as I finished: "Do you really believe that?"

---

5   See chapter 13 of *Church Still Works* (Striving Together Publications, 2009) for statistics on church planting needs.

6   See Ministry127.com and ChurchPlanting127.com for church planting resources.

To her, the gospel was incredible—unbelievable. To have an educated American explaining what seemed like a make-believe story intrigued and perplexed her.

This dear lady did not trust Christ that afternoon, but I've thought of her question a thousand times since: "Do you really believe that?" With over 4.7 billion people who make no profession of Christianity[7] and over 2.8 billion people who have never one time heard the gospel,[8] I'm not sure we are in a good position to answer her question. After all, if we really believed the gospel, wouldn't we be more obedient in fulfilling the Great Commission?

Over the years, one of the greatest strengths of the independent Baptist movement has been missions. With a system as simple as the model found in Acts 13, our missionaries—like our churches—are free of bureaucratic machinery and encouraged to plant indigenous churches. They are sent by a pastor and church who undertake the concern of their spiritual and ministry wellbeing, and they are supported by several churches who pitch in to advance the message of the gospel. It's a win-win for everyone.

This strength of our movement, however, is not impregnable. We can easily become complacent and neglect the needs beyond our front door. Reaching the world with the gospel can only happen through increased fervency and dedication.

---

7   Stats calculated from population and religion percentages listed in the World Fact Book (CIA), a publication from the Central Intelligence Agency, February, 2013, https://www.cia.gov/library/publications/the-world-factbook/index.html.

8   Stats provided by the Joshua Project, joshuaproject.net, February, 2013.

EARNESTLY SEEK REVIVAL

America has been blessed of God with multiple revivals that began in a single church or area and spread nationally. Our prayer for today is for a revival of God's people. "Wilt thou not revive us again: that thy people may rejoice in thee?" (Psalm 85:6).

While we are commanded to preach the Word, we must also live the Word. If we fail in our personal lives, the message of truth with which we have been entrusted will be rejected by a cynical and doubting generation. "Pray for us: for we trust we have a good conscience, in all things willing to live honestly" (Hebrews 13:18).

As my friend, Dr. Wayne Van Gelderen, has pointed out, "If we are going to receive the promise of God's blessing, our whole heartbeat has to be for God's cause."[9] We must earnestly seek revival through prayer, preaching, and repentance toward God and men.

KEEP THE MAIN THING THE MAIN THING

Success in any endeavor is defined by how operations and results compare to the original mission. In the big picture, completion of this mission is all that matters.

Our original mission is clear—God has specifically committed the gospel to our trust (1 Thessalonians 2:4), and He has commanded us to take it to the world. Baseline, authentic ministry is just that— reaching people with the gospel.

I believe that the greatest danger we face as independent Baptists is not that of direct attacks—from within or without—

---

9   March 22, 2012, sermon "Preparing to Pray for Revival," available at fallsbc.org/sermons.

but the danger of distraction. Critics may be able to question or sideline our ministries, but only we silence our witness—at home or around the globe.

It's all too easy to fill our schedules with activity—good, profitable activity—but not experience the real productivity of souls saved and lives changed by the power of the gospel.

The road ahead, if it is a scriptural road, will maintain a tenacious direction on the central mission of the local church—soulwinning and outreach.

Identify Ourselves
Biblically and Wisely

Late in December of every year I carve out some time to plan for the new year. Ideally, I sit in front of a crackling fire and reflect on the past year before preparing for the coming year. Sometimes, however, my planning surroundings are less idyllic. Some years have found my priorities and goals scribbled in a hotel room or perhaps in the waiting room of a hospital.

Regardless of my environment, it is always helpful for me to step back from my normal routines for a fresh perspective. Besides giving me plans for the year ahead, this time is a reset for me in reestablishing direction in my God-given roles.

As I pull out a pen, the first word I write on the top of my yellow pad is "Christian," for this is the first and most vital role in my life. I accepted Jesus Christ as my Saviour on April 5, 1972. By His grace, He was merciful to forgive me and save me on that day.

After "Christian," I list several other God-given roles—husband, father, grandfather, pastor, etc.—leaving space between each to fill in with goals. I then begin to plan the coming year around these words. These identifying roles help me to plan proper scriptural emphasis of my time, talents, and treasure toward that which ultimately would bring glory to God.

Similarly, as a pastor, it has been my privilege to spend nearly thirty years helping new Christians understand the words that identify us as a local Baptist church. I love teaching the position and identity of a New Testament church. Through the years, I have sat in hundreds of homes and explained the basic, fundamental doctrines of the Bible to interested and prospective members. I have written the distinctives of Baptists on napkins and pads of paper, and I have explained what it means to be a church with fundamental doctrine.

Additionally, I explain the identifying monikers "independent fundamental Baptist." The short version goes something like this: "*Independent* means that we are an autonomous local church with Christ as the head of the church. We recognize that He owns the church, and we are directly accountable to Him. We do not function under an ecclesiastical hierarchy. We support our missionaries directly and enjoy hearing them report personally. *Fundamental* means that we believe the basics—the fundamentals—of Christianity. In the same way a basketball coach might teach his players the fundamentals of their sport—ball-handling, passing, shooting, defense, and teamwork—our church believes and teaches the basic truths of the Bible, literally and absolutely.[1] *Baptist* is

---

[1] See *What Is a Biblical Fundamentalist?* Striving Together Publications, 2005, page 6 for a more fleshed-out version of this comparison.

the name that embodies the truths we believe. Baptists believe in salvation through Jesus Christ alone...."

It has always been a joy to me to explain biblical doctrine and the scriptural identity of our church with an open Bible to an eager, receptive new believer.

I am aware, however, that some of these terms are becoming increasingly misunderstood and maligned. While our identifying terms—independent fundamental Baptist—are easily and quickly recognized for what they have historically meant among fellow pastors and core members of our churches, they are becoming challenging in the context of soulwinning and evangelism. Of course, this problem goes back to Chapter 1—the problem of a tarnished name.

WHY WE MUST REAFFIRM THE TRUTH

Because there has been an increase of Internet dialogue and major network reporting on various types of scandals in Christianity—including such occurrences in some independent Baptist churches—it is vital that we identify ourselves biblically and wisely for this generation. This is necessary for the lost we are trying to reach and for sincere Christians who want to know our hearts. (I do understand that there will always be pathological antagonists who have an axe to grind and truly don't want restoration. It seems some people find their identity in constant gossip, malice, and stirring strife on the Internet regarding how they view a person who attends a conservative church.) Although I disagree with the media's approach of casting aspersion on thousands of pastors and about 2.5 million good Christians,[2] I, along with many others, have been burdened for the testimony of our biblical heritage.

Sadly, I have known some "staunch fundamentalists" who were lousy Christians. And, as we have seen in these pages, I have known many who have redefined the word *fundamental* to include much more than doctrine. For many, the word includes personal ideas, strong opinions, and even bizarre viewpoints or practices.

It seems to me that we may be coming to a point as independent Baptists that in a Christlike and positive manner, we reaffirm our biblical doctrine, our Baptist distinctives, and our spiritual practices. I believe we also need great sensitivity in how we identify ourselves to those who are unfamiliar with the historic meaning of "independent fundamental Baptist."

MORE IMPORTANT THAN A LABEL

I'm a believer in labels, and to me, a name says a lot. But Shakespeare raised a valid point when he raised the famous question, "What's in a name? That which we call a rose, By any other name would smell as sweet."[3]

As important as labels and identities may be, a name is only as meaningful as the reality to which it is tied. No label is as vital as the anointing of God. And no term is as essential as the authenticity of the ministry behind it.

I am a Christian and a Baptist by conviction. I make no apology for the scriptural teaching of the autonomy of the church

---

2   *Church Still Works*, (Striving Together Publications, 2009), 14–15
3   *Romeo and Juliet*, edited by William Strunk, Jr. (Houghton Mifflin Company, 1906), 28.

(independent), for the orthodoxy of my faith (fundamental), or for the heritage of my position (Baptist). I do recognize, however, that recent events—from both within and without independent fundamental churches—have caused the three words "independent fundamental Baptist" when used together as an identifying moniker to mean something far different than the early leaders of our movement had in mind as they chose these words. When I'm soulwinning door-to-door in our community or talking to a newer Christian, I have reason to consider what my listener hears when I say I'm the pastor of an "independent fundamental Baptist" church or what he sees if he reads it on our sign by the road.[4] He may be thinking of a tarnished reputation. (Just recently, I spoke with a pastor in the Midwest who described to me the difficulty of using these terms when canvassing in his community in light of the group identity issues related to problems in a nearby church.)

> No label is as vital as the anointing of God. And no term is as essential as the authenticity of the ministry behind it.

Of course, if the listener gives me time, I could explain the history of Baptists, the original intent of the early leaders of our movement, the dictionary definition of my terms…But chances are, he won't give me the time. And, personally, I'm not willing to take this chance. I'd rather be careful now and explain later than explain now and regret later.

---

4   Independent Baptists are not alone in stolen terms. In the book *The Courage to Be Protestant*, David Wells raises the same concern regarding the use of the term *evangelical*. (William B. Eerdmans Publishing Company, 2008), 19–21.

My highest consideration in a conversation with an unsaved person or a new Christian needing the spiritual oversight of a church family is that person's soul. I'll use language he understands until I can help him understand the historical meaning of terms that are precious to me.[5]

CONSIDERING OUR OPTIONS

So what do you do when your terminology seems to be wearing thin, like a tire running out of tread?

I believe first of all, one must check his heart to be sure these questions are not stemming from an insidious root—the fear of man.

An entire generation of Christians is turning away from Bible terms simply because of the fear of man or from a desire to be more acceptable. We must be sure the fear of God always dominates our hearts and our decision processes. Our target in identifying ourselves has never been to appear "cool" or even primarily to be "relative." When considering labels we must remember that the local church belongs to Christ. Ultimately, the titles we choose reflect on His reputation.

As a pastor/teacher, I have lived with a passion to help people understand the Bible. I have taught in conferences and in our

---

5   I am not alone in this approach. In preparing this manuscript, I asked a
     large number of pastors—all of whom are strong independent Baptists
     with a commitment to biblical doctrine and to soulwinning—the question,
     "What vernacular do you use to describe your church when you are out
     soulwinning in your community?" The vast majority (97 percent) used a
     term other than "independent fundamental Baptist," although all of them
     would claim that term as an accurate description of what they believe. Most
     say "Bible-believing Baptist" or "Bible-believing church."

Bible college that we must teach Bible messages that are clearly understood. It is not my job to market the truth by making it more "palatable" to a person by deleting truths that may be doctrinally distasteful. If the Bible or a Bible-based message from a biblical Baptist church offends, then we still must stand for the truth.

When I became a preacher of the gospel, I knew from the outset that the gospel itself is offensive to the fallen nature.[6] I have no delusion that I can preach the gospel accurately and avoid the offense associated with it. On the other hand, I believe there is wisdom in taking an honest look at the offence of a name identity that is being used as a broad brush to the detriment of God's work in solid, loving churches of integrity.

> We must be sure the fear of God always dominates our hearts and our decision processes.

Second, when you have concerns with the perceptions associated with identifying terms, don't choose something just to please the modern generation.

Every few months I have the privilege to teach the "Starting Point" class at our church—a three-week class for newcomers. In our most recent class I taught seventy-five prospective members from a variety of backgrounds. In this class were single moms, a couple who was saved from an Islamic background, a single dad from a Catholic background, and young couples with no religious background at all. As I taught the class, I endeavored to share predominantly biblical terms while defining the DNA of Lancaster

---

6   1 Peter 2:7–8

Baptist Church. I spoke often of the fact that we are a biblical Baptist church. I shared that Baptist churches believe Jesus is the chief Shepherd of the church. We believe that a person at salvation is sealed by the Holy Spirit and that the Bible is our final authority in all matters of faith and practice.

By describing our church as an autonomous, biblical Baptist church, I find the new Christian is benefited in a few important ways: First, his early associated description of our church is the word *biblical*. Second, if he has been influenced by the real problems or the exaggerated issues surrounding the term "IFB,"[7] I believe he will benefit from my decision to direct him to Scriptures and away from confusion.[8]

As spiritual undershepherds, we must consider how to lead our churches to the still water of God's truth and steer clear of the torrents of criticism, malice, and issues that draw people away into destructive lives.

Personally, I find myself describing our church as a Bible-based Baptist church that is unaffiliated from a denomination. Baptist distinctives have always taught that Baptists are autonomous. In the last seventy or eighty years we have used the term "independent" to describe our autonomous position. But either word means essentially the same thing. When explaining our position to a new convert, one friend tells them, "We are not like Safeway [a chain grocery story]. We are like the mom and pop store on the corner."

---

7   I never heard the term "IFB" in a grouping or branding sense until a couple of years ago. It was apparently coined and used by people who were hurt or disappointed by abuse in independent churches, and it was used more of spite than respect.

8   We know that God is not the author of this confusion (1 Corinthians 14:33), and we know that He does not send fear into men's hearts; but His desire is to give power, love, and a sound mind (2 Timothy 1:7).

(I think it is relevant to remember that even the name "independent Baptist" was derived by men who were solidly Baptist but who felt their group identities were not pleasing to Christ because of compromise. Most of us don't consider Lee Roberson or G. B. Vick insecure men who were just trying to please men with a new label! These were men of good conscience and pure doctrine who did not want to give an uncertain sound as it related to their ministry.)

Incidentally, it may be that the term independent fundamental Baptist is less a stumbling block in certain areas of the country. A Barna study recently concluded that several areas of the country are still very "biblically minded."[9] I would suppose that in parts of Tennessee the name Baptist and the basic teachings of the Bible are more clearly understood than they are here in Southern California. But even in the most traditionally Christian parts of the nation, it is becoming more needful to identify ourselves biblically and wisely for those who do not understand our biblical distinctives.

POTENTIAL RESPONSES

There's no doubt in my mind that our culture and the media in particular will portray biblically based churches as "out of touch" or "dangerous" in the days ahead, and I believe it's important that we position ourselves biblically and rightly in this generation. I'm praying God will use us again to engage our perverse nation with the absolute truths of Christ.

---

9   "Bible-Minded Cities," http://cities.barna.org/americas-most-and-least-bible-minded-cities-2/, accessed 3/20/13.

As I've shared the material in this book with friends in the ministry and asked for their perspective on the current landscape of our movement, many have fully identified with these concerns. From my experiences and theirs, it seems there are three categorical responses to discussion on imbalances within our movement and the issue of how we identify ourselves. Perhaps your response likewise fits into one of the categories below.

Unconcerned

Some dismiss these issues entirely. They simply don't have interest in the discussion.

Some of my friends over sixty are coming down the homestretch of their ministry, and they don't want to mess with semantics. Their general attitude is, "The current label has done me well thus far." If this describes you, I'd ask you to consider the testimony of Christ and the future of this movement in the days ahead. My generation of preachers is generally unaware that tomorrow's positions are being developed by young pastors who are on the Internet and blogs. Young leaders *need* you in this discussion. They are talking whether you and I join them or not. So rather than ignore the issue, I encourage you to engage.

Concerned

Some pastors acknowledge our current identity challenges but have made no adjustments in the way they introduce their ministry or position. Out of love for and loyalty to our heritage, their heart response is, "These are good thoughts, but I like the name."

I love the historic meaning of our name as well. Most of us will continue to use the term independent Baptist in one context or another. In fact, I have several good friends whose churches are actually named "Independent Baptist Church."

But for those who will continue to use the word in a public venue it will be more and more important to define the term scripturally and lovingly within our communities. Perhaps you could include on your church website a clear explanation of your definitions. You must do a better job of positioning yourself in your community than the "haters" do of positioning you. And we must be ready always with an answer for those who will try to lump us in with people we would never have in our own pulpits.

Some men might want to refer to themselves with different vernacular. If this is you, I encourage you to proceed with prayer. There is much to take into consideration as you choose words to identify yourself. Be wise and cautious, and seek counsel from others who love the historic principles of our movement and are solid in their commitment to truth.

While I continue to identify myself among pastors and fellow independent Baptists as an independent fundamental Baptist, when speaking in my community or to the press who are not familiar with the historic meaning of these words, I refer to myself as a biblical Baptist who is unaffiliated from a nationally organized group. I explain that we are a church that derives our doctrine and practice not from a camp or religious culture, but from scriptural guidelines.

Already changed affiliations

Some readers have left more than a name. You've not only left the "IFB," but you've identified with another group or philosophy. To you, I want to say that I love you as a brother in Christ. If you are preaching the gospel, seeking to see souls saved, and proclaiming the truth of God's Word, you are not my enemy.

To the extent that your new group identity may create uncertainty of your stand doctrinally, I would lovingly encourage you to be sensitive to the Holy Spirit. Otherwise, I truly wish you God's best.

CAN A GOOD NAME BE MISUNDERSTOOD?

My friend, R. B. Ouellette, goes by his initials, but his real name is René Bach. His parents chose this name for good reasons. René was the name of his dad's French teacher in Bible college. It means "born again." His dad had just recently been saved, so the meaning of this name, combined with this man who helped his dad grow in the Lord, held special significance to him.

Actually, René is a French name. When it is used for a boy, there is only one *e* at the end, and when it is used for a girl, there are two. But shortly after R. B. began pastoring, he learned that most Americans don't get the one *e* rule for his name. In fact, they thought his wife was the pastor!

When René began preaching occasionally for other churches, pastors told him they found it awkward to put his name on flyers used to promote the meetings.

You might suggest that he could use his middle name. That one, too, seemed unlikely. His middle name is Bach—his mother's maiden name.

As you know now, he chose to go by his initials—R. B. Yet, his family still calls him René. In fact, he never legally changed his name; he simply changed how he chose to project himself to those who wouldn't understand.

I am at a similar place regarding the name "independent fundamental Baptist." I love this name, and many of us understand its significance. When speaking with anyone who understands its historic meaning, I gladly identify myself as an independent fundamental Baptist. But for those who don't share my context or understanding, *I often refer to myself as a "biblical or unaffiliated Baptist."*

THE ULTIMATE IDENTIFICATION

One of my favorite illustrations to share in our Starting Point class is that of a church I once preached at in Cebu City, Philippines. The church's name is the Bible Baptist Church. (This is actually a church planted by the same Bob Hughes whom I mentioned in Chapter 8.)

On the side of the church building is a large sign that reads, "What the Bible says." You can get into a taxi anywhere in Cebu City and say, "Take me to a church that will tell me what the Bible says." The driver will take you immediately to the Bible Baptist Church.

As I relate this story to our new members, I share that my heart's desire is to pastor a church that is known for teaching *what the Bible says*!

The blessing of ministry does not flow through group identity. The blessing flows from God alone, to yielded vessels and local churches who are faithful to proclaim "what the Bible says." If enough of us pastors and church leaders will humble ourselves and seek His face, He will hear... He will forgive, and He will heal. I long for a clear identification with Christ personally, and the powerful anointing of God on the church I pastor. One man, and one church at a time, God can and will graciously renew us in His ministry.

> My heart's desire is to pastor a church that is known for teaching what the Bible says!

No pastor or Christian leader is perfect, but we should all be growing on this journey of ministry. As we strive to identify ourselves with Christ and His Word and obey the leadership of the Holy Spirit, I believe the road ahead will lead us to the One who will say, "Well done, thou good and faithful servant."

W E'VE COVERED A LOT OF ground in these pages. Historically, doctrinally, positionally, practically—we've examined a wide range of topics and pointed out a number of steps we can take for authentic ministry on the road ahead.

As we conclude, let's take a quick look at the steps we've covered from a different perspective. Briefly, let's take to the sky for an aerial panoramic view:

Step 1: Understand the need for a good name. You and I have the privilege to bear the name of Christ as we serve. Because the local church belongs to Him and because what we do is a direct reflection on His reputation, we must live with integrity, serve with authenticity, and seek revival.

Step 2: Remain steadfast to the truth. No forward steps of ministry will be ultimately blessed if we forsake truth in the process.

Step 3: Remember our heritage. The way forward is best understood by examining the patterns of the past—especially in seeing the courageous stand men of earlier generations have taken for the truths of the New Testament local church.

Step 4: Enjoy biblical fellowship. We ambush ourselves when we form "camps" around personalities and places rather than encouraging each other as fellow soldiers on the path of truth.

Step 5: Confront false teaching and sin. One of the biggest challenges we face in witnessing today is the proliferation of church leaders who have lived immoral or biblically inconsistent lives. In this day of compromise, we need men with grace and courage to take the right stand in the right way.

Step 6: Correct imbalances in ministry. The target in every area of ministry is to be like Jesus—full of grace and truth. Those who serve in the name of Christ must make Jesus their goal, avoid the pitfalls of pride that are so prevalent in ministry, and serve with humility and personal purity.

Step 7: Be grace givers. We must be careful to strive together for the truth rather than fight one another over slight differences. When we agree on 99.9 percent of our practices, we would be wisest to support one another with Romans 14 grace.

Step 8: Engage younger pastors in ministry conversations. Honest questions and transparent answers are vital marks of authenticity—especially when it comes to ministry. The ideas, observations, and questions of younger pastors should be taken seriously and engaged with wisdom and humility. We need these young leaders in our ranks.

Step 9: Return to soulwinning and outreach. Christ gave the local church one mission—reach the world with the gospel. If we will make a difference in this generation, we must return to the biblical priorities of soulwinning, discipleship, and church planting.

Step 10: Identify ourselves biblically and wisely. We serve in a hostile culture, and we must be ready to give every man an answer for the hope we preach. Because we carry the name of Christ, we must position ourselves biblically and rightly in this generation.

In all of these areas, I am still desiring God's grace to mold and make me into a better servant for Him. I want the Holy Spirit to continue convicting, prompting, and working in my heart as I continue forward for Him.

Anyone who travels by air on a regular basis is bound to encounter occasional turbulence. Some flights may encounter brief bumps; some may have longer periods of rough air; others may include more desperate moments while the plane pitches and tips.

In every flight in which I've experienced turbulence, there is one statement that gives me assurance. It is when the pilot acknowledges that he knows it's rough and then says, "We're making adjustments up here in the cockpit."

That one statement calms my nerves and relaxes my muscles. I have no idea what kind of adjustments the pilot is making, but I'm thankful he isn't ignoring the signs of imbalance.

So it is in ministry. Any preacher who has served almost any length of time has encountered turbulence. The storms of ministry come from within and without. Some are merely uncomfortable; others threaten to drive us far off course. In either case, we must be proactive in making adjustments as we navigate towards our destination.

Thankfully, we are not without help or guidance in these seasons. Even as the pilot has a manual on which to base his decisions, we have been given God's Word. Like the pilot's manual, it does not describe every possible scenario the winds of change or adversity may bring, but it gives us every needed principle on which information we must consider and which dynamics of our lives and ministries can be adjusted. Furthermore, we have a resource available even greater—the very wisdom of God and the direction of His Spirit.

I don't know what turbulence we may face in the days ahead, but I do know that God has put at our disposal every resource we need to press forward for Him. It is our responsibility, however, to be sensitive to His Spirit and to be willing to make adjustments in the cockpit.

I'm enjoying the journey of ministry, but I especially look forward to the end of the trip when the skies part and I enter the presence of my Lord. When today's road ahead becomes yesterday's record of God's faithfulness, I'll be thankful for any adjustment I made to press forward for my Lord.

Ours is the privilege to lift up the cross and exalt the name of Jesus through His local church. This is no small task, but neither is there a small reward for those who will undertake the journey in the power of the Holy Spirit.

I cannot stress enough that the highest purpose of this book is to exalt the Lord Jesus Christ. The investment of time for this project would be unwise were it just about man-made issues and identities.

While biblical Baptist churches must continue to stand against the sin of the culture and overcome the identity challenges mentioned in this book, I believe there are still great victories awaiting those who humbly and patiently lift up the cross and rightly divide the Word.

We are commanded that Jesus alone is to receive glory in the church (Ephesians 3:21). And when local church pastors who are referred to as stars in Revelation 3 are lost in semantics, arguments, and hurtful identity discussions, it distracts us from our real job— to deflect the glory and praise to the Lord Jesus Christ.

Despite the fact that a number of churches have shifted direction and are only a shadow of what they used to be, there are many young pastors stepping into older churches and seeing a complete rebound through soulwinning and discipleship. We continue to see good numbers of young couples going to mission fields and there is a resurging interest in church planting.

Just this past week, as I completed this book, I spoke to pastors in their thirties and forties who have recently experienced record attendances in Nevada, California, Connecticut, Florida, and Washington state. All of these pastors are resisting the pluralism and ecumenical compromise of the day and are also resistant toward pragmatism and strife. They are men who simply desire to be used of God and are seeing souls come to Christ weekly.

God is still honoring His Word and still working through yielded men. I encourage you to lift up the cross. I encourage you to "buy the truth and sell it not" (Proverbs 23:23). I challenge you to learn and love our Baptist heritage. I ask you to be thankful for the freedom and strengths of autonomy. And, I remind you that for those who seek biblically authentic ministry, the road ahead will be blessed by the Lord according to His might and power.

I have no misconception that the road ahead for biblical Baptist churches will be easy, but I believe the journey and the destination can and will be glorious as we walk with Christ and look unto Him as the author and finisher of our faith. Titles, movements, and groups fade into eternity. But what we do today through the New Testament local church under the leadership of Christ has eternal value. Jesus said it Himself: "…I will build my church; and the gates of hell shall not prevail against it" (Matthew 16:18).

IF THIS BOOK HAS BEEN a blessing to you; if you identify with the spirit in which it was written; if your heart is to be an autonomous biblical Baptist with a firm stand, gracious spirit, and heart for soulwinning and missions; if you lead in a ministry that has implemented (and plans to continue to uphold) policies that discourage the tarnishing of our testimony, I invite you to sign in at the following page:

ministry127.com/theroadahead

Here, with other biblical Baptists, you can acknowledge the need for balance, commit to pray for revival, and agree to work toward these goals. See you there!

On the Late Massacre in Piedmont

THE POET JOHN MILTON HONORED the brave, uncompromising courage of the Waldenses with a now-famous sonnet:

On the Late Massacre in Piedmont

Avenge, O Lord, thy slaughtered saints, whose bones
Lie scattered on the Alpine mountains cold,
Even them who kept thy truth so pure of old,
When all our fathers worshiped stocks and stones;
Forget not: in thy book record their groans
Who were thy sheep and in their ancient fold
Slain by the bloody Piedmontese that rolled
Mother with infant down the rocks. Their moans
The vales redoubled to the hills, and they
To Heaven. Their martyred blood and ashes sow
O'er all th' Italian fields where still doth sway
The triple tyrant; that from these may grow
A hundredfold, who having learnt thy way
Early may fly the Babylonian woe.

Ten Marks of Imbalance
in Ministry

L EADING IN MINISTRY IS LIKE walking a tightrope. Not only does it require delicate balance, but the stakes are high if we slip.

As spiritual leaders, it is our responsibility to walk with balance. Ephesians 5:15 puts it succinctly—"walk circumspectly." But if we were to get off balance, what would it look like? The infographic on the next page lists the ten marks of imbalance in ministry covered in chapter 6 of this book. These can describe a leader personally, or a ministry in general. Either way, the results are tragic.

Any of these imbalances—and especially the pride that drives them—can creep up on us with such stealth as to make the imbalance imperceptible in the beginning. For this reason, we must daily, constantly look to the Holy Spirit for conviction, cleansing, and power.

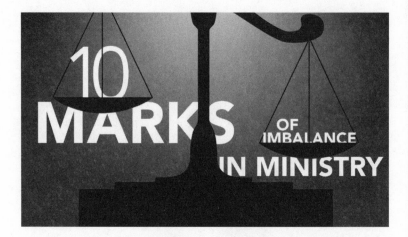

10 MARKS OF IMBALANCE IN MINISTRY

ANGER

Angry preaching is often a sign of an insecure pastor who attempts to motivate through guilt and shame rather than relying on the powerful grace of God.

JAMES 1:20

CONCERN FOR IMAGE OVER INTEGRITY

Any form of protecting image over integrity—ignoring sin, hiding crime, or placing more importance on appearance than substance—is pride. It doesn't protect the name of Christ; it tarnishes His name.

JAMES 4:10

PRIDE IN NUMBERS

If we shift our focus from God's glory and compete (even subconsciously) with other ministries to be the biggest, greatest, fastest growing, or any other superlative, we cut ourselves off from God's grace.

2 CORINTHIANS 10:12

PRIDE IN MEN

Every time we pride ourselves in our associations with men, institutions, or issues, we grieve the only One who grants true empowerment—the Holy Spirit of God.

1 CORINTHIANS 3:4

PRIDE IN STANDARDS

If a standard is based upon a biblical conviction and it helps us to be more Christlike, all the glory should go to Christ. But when we are proud of ourselves and our standards, we glorify ourselves.

2 CORINTHIANS 10:17

LITTLE OR NO ACCOUNTABILITY WITHIN LEADERSHIP

Sin will always find the darkest corner from which to work. It lurks in lives and systems that shy from biblical accountability.

JAMES 5:16, 19–20

UNBIBLICAL PREACHING

One of the most tragic mistakes we make is to elevate personal opinions to a doctrinal level or to fill our sermons with stories rather than Scripture. Nothing can replace the contextual, expository preaching of God's Word.

2 TIMOTHY 2:15

LACK OF GRACE

Our lives and our ministries are to be showcases that illuminate God's grace. How tragic when we preach salvation by grace but live and lead in a manner that denies grace.

PHILIPPIANS 2:13

PRIDE IN POSITION

We should be thankful to take our place in a long legacy of men who have studied God's Word and stood for Bible truth; but we dare not become prideful in this position. We are what we are only by God's grace.

1 CORINTHIANS 15:10

MISPLACED IDENTITY

Do we value ourselves based on the number of hours we work or the number of people in our Sunday school class? If so, we will be on a fruitless and frustrating treadmill seeking for approval that we will never fully find.

EPHESIANS 1:6

Instructions for American Servicemen in Britain, 1942

IN THE CITY OF LONDON there is a museum between St. James Park and the river Thames called "Churchill's War Rooms." Several years ago, I had the privilege of visiting this museum with my family, and in it, I found a treasure of a book: *Instructions for American Servicemen in Britain.* This small volume was published in 1942 as our military joined the Allied Forces in Great Britain.

Written at a time when American patriotism flourished, the United States War Department gave sage advice to our young men regarding tempering American pride with wise cooperation in serving with our allies. As I read these instructions, I immediately noticed how closely several of them relate to our roles as pastors in the spiritual battle. Here are a few excerpts from the book.

Replace the enemy name "Hitler" in the following paragraphs with the name of our spiritual enemy "Satan"; replace "America" and "Britain" with your name and that of other Christian servants; when you do, you have a good picture of why we must extend grace one towards another.

Instructions for American Servicemen in Britain

You are going to Great Britain as part of an Allied offensive—to meet Hitler and beat him on his own ground.... America and Britain are allies. Hitler knows that they are both powerful countries, tough and resourceful. He knows that they, with the other United Nations, mean his crushing defeat in the end.

So it is only common sense to understand that the first and major duty Hitler has given his propaganda chiefs is to separate Britain and America and spread distrust between them....

No Time to Fight Old Wars

If you come from an Irish-American family, you may think of the English as persecutors of the Irish, or you may think of them as enemy Redcoats who fought against us in the American Revolution and the War of 1812. But there is no time today to fight old wars over again or bring up old grievances. Don't worry about which side our grandfathers fought on in the Civil War, because it doesn't mean anything now.

Don't Be a Show Off

The British dislike bragging and showing off....Use common sense, and don't rub [the British "Tommy"] the wrong way.

The British Are Tough

Sixty thousand British civilians—men, women, and children—have died under bombs, and yet the morale of the British is unbreakable and high. A nation doesn't come through that if it doesn't have plain, common guts. The British are tough, strong people, and good allies.

You won't be able to tell the British much about "taking it." They are not particularly interested in taking it any more. They are far more interested in getting together in solid friendship with us, so that we can all start dishing it out to Hitler.

Keep Out of Arguments

...Look, listen, and learn before you start telling the British how much better we do things.... When you find differences between the British and American ways of doing things, there is usually a good reason for them....

The British don't know how to make a good cup of coffee. You don't know how to make a good cup of tea. It's an even swap....

Use common sense on all occasions. By your conduct you have great power to bring about a better understanding between the two countries after the war is over.... In your dealings with them, let this be your slogan:

It is always impolite to criticize your hosts; it is militarily stupid to criticize your allies.

—United States War Department, *Instructions for American Servicemen in Britain,* 1942 (Republished by Bodleian Library, University of Oxford, 2004). Also available through Amazon.com.

Concerns and Hopes
for Preachers

S OME TIME AGO, A YOUNG PASTOR asked me a thought-provoking question: "What do you see that concerns or encourages you in younger pastors?"

I was encouraged by the question itself, and I pondered it for the next few days. I still consider myself a "younger pastor" and gladly learn from others, but perhaps because I've crossed the line of fifty, I feel old enough to answer the question.

Here are a few thoughts:

For younger preachers

I get concerned when a young preacher has a sarcastic attitude toward most older pastors in ministry.

I get hopeful when he has a general sense of respect and fellowship with older pastors.

I get concerned when a young preacher attempts to quickly copy any new fad or method from a mega church that appears successful.

I get hopeful when a young preacher "tries the spirits to see whether they be of God" (1 John 4:1).

I get concerned when a young preacher has an argumentative spirit.

I get hopeful when a young preacher approaches me with a sincere heart, even when his ideas are different than mine.

I get concerned when a young preacher constantly tweets and links to authors or pastors who are not cessationists, who drink alcohol, and who are staunch Calvinists.

I am hopeful and encouraged when a young preacher tweets Scripture or tells how he recently led someone to Christ.

I get concerned when a young preacher is primarily influenced by web-based ministry.

I get hopeful when a young preacher is consistent in his Bible reading and his heart burns within him when the Bible is soundly preached.

I get concerned when a young preacher's questions rarely revolve around doctrine or theology.

I am blessed by young preachers who have a heart for God and His truth and inquire about how to better serve Him.

I get concerned when a young preacher reads only "best-selling church growth" books.

I am blessed by young preachers who read Christian classics, who study doctrine, and who rightly divide the Word of truth.

I get concerned with a young preacher whose modern methods overshadow the message and whose love of culture crowds out the gospel of Christ.

I am encouraged by young preachers who are careful that Christ and His Word are truly preeminent in ministry.

I get concerned when a young preacher is reacting against an angry, absent, or abusive authority figure as he crafts his ministry philosophy.

I get hopeful when his philosophy is derived from a causative and definite walk with God.

I get concerned when a young preacher (on the right or left) gets critical. Many young "progressives" claim they are leaving a "fundamental context" because they sense harshness in our ranks. Yet, many of these who are moving positions are equally caustic in their spirit to those who are on the same old path.

I get encouraged when any Christian displays a Christlike spirit.

I get concerned when a young preacher spends excessive time on social network sites.

I get hopeful when young preachers are out in the community, conducting outreach and discipleship, and spending time with people who need personal ministry.

I get concerned when a young preacher wants to invest his time only with a certain segment of the "beautiful people" in society.

I am encouraged by young pastors who have a heart for the hurting, the poor, and the elderly.

I get concerned when a young preacher naïvely believes that most pastors in the group he grew up in are weird or wrong and that other groups have all the "cool" or "more balanced" leadership.

I get hopeful when preachers admit that every group has inherent problems because of our sin nature and that no one group is ever perfectly balanced or without sin.

For older preachers

I get concerned when older preachers view all those with a question as "in rebellion."

It encourages me to see older preachers take time with younger preachers.

I get concerned when older preachers won't admit the shortcomings of our generation of leadership.

I get encouraged when older preachers say, "Here are some mistakes we made; try not to make them."

I get concerned when older preachers elevate preference to the place of doctrine.

I am hopeful when an older preacher admits that his preferences are simply preferences. "Nothing in the Bible says a man must wear a tie (etc.), but here is why I prefer doing it that way." (See Romans 14.)

I get concerned when older preachers won't admit that leaders in other circles do "anything right."

I get hopeful when an older preacher kindly disagrees with another leader or group but credits them for their efforts in some area (such as fighting abortion).

I get concerned when older preachers stake loyalty to a college or institution, even when the philosophy of that institution no longer produces passionate Christian servants.

I get encouraged when older preachers follow principle and seek revival with like-minded men who may be from a different college background.

I get concerned when older preachers speak only about who they saw come to Christ decades ago.

I am encouraged by older preachers who have the spirit of Caleb and are still reaching out with the gospel.

I get concerned when older preachers preach against gossip and division in the church, but read negative and gossipy blogs and share that information with their churches and friends.

I am encouraged when older pastors take the "high road" and refuse to lend their ear to non-fruit-bearing trash peddlers.

I get concerned when older preachers assume any slight variances in a church schedule or method is always indicative that a younger preacher is on a "slippery slope."

I am thankful for older preachers who allow for growth and even mistakes in the lives of developing leaders. It is worthy of noting that some of the greatest "fundamental" leaders I have known were quite innovative. While some did not prefer such methods, most did not deem those who used these methods as "liberal." Dr. Curtis Hutson encouraged me to use a two-service schedule on Sunday mornings, and Dr. Tom Malone encouraged me to use screens in our services; still others were critical of both.

I get concerned when older preachers mellow to the point of leaving their once firmly proclaimed distinctives.

I am grateful for consistent, gracious leaders who walk in truth, contend for the faith, and love the brethren.

I have had the privilege of knowing and receiving personal influence from some of the greatest leaders of the previous generation. They weren't perfect, but their examples remind us to, regardless of our age, faithfully preach the gospel, lovingly invest in others, and graciously live for Christ.

Sample Policies for Local Church Ministries

Throughout this book, I've mentioned the importance of having clear ministry policies that honor the Lord and protect the integrity of the local church. Throughout the years, our church has developed several hundred pages of such policies. Some are primarily logistical, created for consistency across our ministry. But many are written primarily to uphold and promote integrity—for each staff member or volunteer, for the church itself, and to protect those we are privileged to serve.

Following are a few such procedures from the policy manual of Lancaster Baptist Church.

- Working with Children
- Biblical Counseling
- Reporting of a Breach of Staff Policies or a Moral Failure
- Whistle-Blower Policy

SUBJECT
Working with Children

Purpose

The purpose of this policy shall be to develop guidelines for the personal conduct of Ministry employees and volunteers whose service involves ministering to children.

Policy

It is the policy of the Ministry that we avoid any negligence in the fulfillment of our duty when working with children.

Procedures

General

1. Every worker, whose service involves ministering to children, must read and abide by the philosophy set forth in the Lancaster Baptist Church Children's Ministries Policies and Procedures and by the Leadership Requirements of the Ministry.

2. Any worker unwilling to adhere to these guidelines will not be permitted to work with children. The glory of God and the integrity of the Ministry cannot suffer the potential consequences from an individual who is insensitive to the risks which are assumed on his behalf.

3. The honorable intentions of godly and dedicated Christians are not being questioned. However, the best intentions are not sufficient protection against hostile accusations against the Ministry or its workers.

Enlistment of Help

1. All workers who come into contact with children in the performance of their duties must complete a Lancaster Baptist Church Personnel Interview Form and be cleared through proper channels before ever being enlisted as a volunteer. All staff members must complete a Staff Personnel Interview Form. Individuals who have been accused or convicted of lewd acts or violence and/or are included in registries, such as "Megan's Law," cannot work with children or be involved in any aspect (planning, transportation, etc.) of the children's ministries of Lancaster Baptist Church.

2. Unless specifically authorized by the appropriate Department Director, all individuals desiring to work with children must be faithful members of Lancaster Baptist Church for a minimum of six (6) months.

Supervision of Children

Ministry volunteers and employees must never be alone with a child in a classroom, restroom, playground, office, counseling area, car, or bus. Two workers must be present with children at all times, and one worker must be at least eighteen (18) years of age or older.

Discipline

1. Ministry employees and volunteers are strictly prohibited from paddling a child.

2. Ministry employees and volunteers are strictly prohibited from physically striking a child.

206 || THE ROAD AHEAD

3. Ministry employees and volunteers are strictly prohibited from physically controlling a child in such a way as to bruise or inflict injury in any way.

4. When verbally reprimanding a child, Ministry employees and volunteers must control both the volume and tone of their voices. The use of slang, demeaning or racially interpreted words or phrases is strictly prohibited.

5. When young children or older students become disruptive, disobedient, or defiant, the worker's responsibility is to protect other children from harm and isolate the disruptive child as quickly as possible. Whenever possible, workers are to deal with disruptions jointly with another adult.

Contact

1. Male workers should abide by a no-touch policy when working with children; female workers must make sure that all physical contact with children is appropriate and could not be misconstrued in any way. Misunderstandings easily occur when an adult affectionately hugs and kisses children.

2. The appropriate supervisor must be informed of any problems or incidents with children that have required physical control. Careful documentation must be made of the incident and the action taken.

3. The testimony of the Lord and the integrity of the Ministry must be maintained at all costs. Therefore, the inappropriate actions of a co-worker must be reported to the appropriate supervisor immediately. This includes any actions or statements which may be viewed with suspicion.

Awareness and Observation

1. Children must never be left alone in classrooms, restrooms, playgrounds, offices, counseling areas, or on buses. Children should be in a worker's line of sight at all times.
2. No child should be allowed to freely roam the property. All children must be in the place where their particular activity is being conducted.
3. Children from birth through sixth grade must be taken to a class and picked up by an authorized individual.

Restroom Procedures

1. Two workers must be present in the room when a child's diaper is changed. Only a female worker may actually change a child's diaper.
2. When taking children to the restroom, two workers must always be present, one of whom must be an adult.
3. Only a female worker will assist a preschool-aged child in the restroom.

Documentation

1. When a disruptive child is corrected and the situation resolved, all workers are to document their actions in writing on the Lancaster Baptist Church Accident/Incident Report.
2. In case of an accident, an Accident/Incident Report shall be completed immediately.
3. Accident/Incident Reports are to be turned in to the appropriate supervisor immediately and forwarded to the Ministry head.

Mandatory Reporting

1. California law states that church volunteers and staff are required to report "reasonable suspicion" of physical abuse, sexual abuse, or neglect taking place in the life of a child. Lancaster Baptist Church practices mandatory reporting according to the California state law. Any accusation against a church worker made by a child will be reported to the authorities.

2. In the case of a report being filed, the volunteer/staff member filing the report will be notified by the office of the Children's Pastor within 24 hours of the notification to the Los Angeles Children's Protective Services. The date and time of contact will be recorded on the original incident report.

SUBJECT
Biblical Counseling

Purpose

The purpose of this twofold policy is to ensure that all employees of the Ministry understand the guidelines for counseling others and to establish safeguards to protect the Ministry.

Policy

It is the policy of the Ministry that all counseling be done within the guidelines prescribed by the Ministry.

Procedures

1. All counseling will be done on the church campus.

2. Only those who are specifically appointed by the Senior Pastor to do counseling shall do counseling for the

Ministry. Counseling, for the purpose of this policy, means meeting in an office or at Ministry facilities for a scheduled purpose of advising someone with respect to his/her problems and questions. Though all employees may be asked, from time to time, to "counsel" a church member in a specific matter, only the pastoral staff or those appointed by the Senior Pastor shall counsel others in personal areas or on an official basis. These areas include, but are not limited to, marriage, career, etc.

3. Appointed counselors will read, agree to, and sign the Counseling Agreement guidelines. Appointed counselors will obtain a signed Ministry Consent to Counsel Document from each counselee. This document will be kept in the counselee's folder.

4. Ministry staff members will not counsel members of another church without written permission from their pastors and a signed Ministry Consent to Counsel Document. This document will be kept in the counselee's folder.

5. The pastoral staff and other male staff of the Ministry will not counsel ladies of the Ministry. If there is a question needing to be answered for a lady in the church, specifically by a pastor, then a church secretary will sit immediately outside the office while the pastoral staff or male staff members speaks to the lady about the situation and refers her to one of the lady counselors from our staff or to one of the pastors' wives. The counselor's door shall remain open.

6. All counseling sessions shall be documented and meticulous notes of each counseling session will be taken. The exact verses shared should be written; comments made by those you've counseled should be listed, as well. These records become a legal document and should be filed in the counselee's files. All notes will be filed and locked away to maintain confidentiality.

7. All counseling shall remain confidential. No staff member may share with another staff member the nature of a counseling session. All counseling is to be confidential, with the exception of the area of child molestation. All admissions to child molestation or any other form of child abuse shall be reported to the police immediately.

8. No staff member will counsel anyone who is suicidal without recommending a medical evaluation for that individual.

9. Counselors shall not have prolonged counseling sessions with those who are not faithful to church services.

COUNSELING AGREEMENT

All counseling done by anyone associated with the Ministry shall be spiritually and biblically based. As a religious counselor for the church, I hereby agree to abide by the following rules:

1. I will be selective as to whom I begin counseling.
2. I will not make claims of providing "secular" counseling and will not perform purely secular functions.

3. I will not hold myself out as a psychotherapist or professional, medical, or psychiatric counselor.

4. I will not imply that I have qualifications which I do not have.

5. I will not use or imply the use of state regulated professional titles such as "licensed professional counselor," "clinical social worker," or "pastoral counselor," unless I am licensed to do so.

6. I will take necessary precautions to insure the confidentiality of the counseling session.

7. I will keep extensive notes of all counseling sessions, including the problem presented and the spiritual advice given. For the purpose of confidentiality, I will keep these records separate and secure.

8. I will not go into a private place with a child alone.

9. I will not go into a child's home while the parents are absent.

10. I will not counsel a child unless accompanied by another adult.

11. I will not counsel members of the opposite sex unless accompanied by a staff member of the opposite sex.

12. I will not have any personal relationship outside of the counseling context with a person I am counseling.

13. I will not coerce anyone into beginning or continuing counseling sessions.

14. I will make notes documenting any allegations of child abuse, or other abuse, which surface during counseling and my observation of any physical injuries, including dates and places. If appropriate, I will urge the counseled person to contact the authorities. If a child states they have been abused, I will call the police.

15. If I find that a counseled person has a serious problem requiring professional treatment, I will immediately refer the

person to a professional, medical, or psychiatric counselor with specialized training.

16. I will not counsel a person for more than six months without the approval of the Senior Pastor.

17. I will avoid strictly psychiatric diagnosis and interventions.

18. I will emphasize the biblical and spiritual dimensions of the religious counseling in any verbal or written descriptions of my counseling services.

19. I will begin every counseling session by explaining that I am not a professional counselor and that I am a spiritual advisor whose advice will be biblically based.

20. I will always refer to the Bible as the source of my advice and read relevant Scripture during each counseling session. I will assign Scripture reading to the counselee.

21. I will pray at least once during every counseling session asking God to give me wisdom during the counseling session being totally dependent upon Him and His Word.

22. I will never give any advice that is contrary to the Bible regardless of the circumstances or situation involved.

As a religious counselor for the church, I hereby agree to submit the following information:

A. Transcripts from all institutions of higher learning.

B. Authorization for Release of Information.

C. Authorization for Criminal Record Check.

Date: _____ Signature: _____

SUBJECT
Reporting of a Breach of Staff Policies or a Moral Failure

Policy

It is the policy of Lancaster Baptist Church that all matters in life be dealt with decently and in order according to biblical standards. Where a breach of staff policy or a moral failure occurs, it is the policy of Lancaster Baptist Church that the matter be dealt with according to the principles set forth in Matthew 18.

Procedures

1. Where a personal grievance arises between staff members, it is expected that the staff members confront one another in the spirit of Matthew 18 for the purpose of restoration. Staff members should never gossip with others not involved in the problem or involved with a solution in the matter.

2. Where the issue that arises cannot be dealt with amongst the individual staff members involved, the staff members should bring the issue to the attention of a pastoral staff member and seek his help in resolving the issue.

3. In a situation where a staff member observes another staff member committing a moral sin (such as swearing, improper contact with the opposite gender, pornographic viewing, stealing, etc.) the staff member observing the situation shall report the situation to his or her Team Leader immediately. The Team Leader shall then bring the situation to the attention of the Senior Pastor who shall review the case and discipline according to the Ministry's Staff Discipline policy.

4. If a situation arises where a staff member is observed in a moral sin that necessitates mandatory reporting, the staff

member observing the situation is bound by the policies of Lancaster Baptist Church to inform the appropriate authorities immediately. The situation should also be brought to the attention of their Team Leader; the Team Leader should then bring the matter to the attention of the Senior Pastor.

5. Where a staff member observes a Team Leader or deacon committing a moral sin, the situation shall immediately be reported to the Senior Pastor who shall review the case and discipline according to the Ministry's Staff Discipline policy.

6. Where a staff member observes the Senior Pastor or a member of his immediate family committing a moral sin, the situation shall immediately be reported to a deacon who shall review the case and discipline according to the Ministry's Church constitution.

7. Appropriate corrective action will be taken, if necessary, and findings will be communicated back to the reporting staff member and the Team Leader by the Senior Pastor or the Deacon Board.

SUBJECT
Whistle-Blower Policy

Policy

If any employee, board member, consultant, or volunteer reasonably believes that some policy, practice, or activity of Lancaster Baptist Church ("Ministry") is in violation of the law, a written complaint may be filed by that employee with the Senior Pastor, Leadership Team Member, or the Chairman of the Church Audit Committee.

It is the intent of the Ministry to adhere to all laws and regulations that apply to the Ministry, and the underlying purpose of this Policy is to support the Ministry's goal of legal compliance. The support of all employees, board members, consultants and volunteers is necessary to achieving compliance with various laws and regulations. In keeping with the policy of maintaining the highest standards of conduct and ethics, the Ministry will investigate any suspected fraudulent or dishonest use or misuse of the Ministry's resources or property by staff, board members, consultants or volunteers. Further, the Ministry is committed to maintaining the highest standards of conduct and ethical behavior and promotes a working environment that values respect, fairness, and integrity. All employees, board members, consultants and volunteers shall act with honesty, integrity, and openness in all their dealings as representatives of the Ministry. Failure to follow these standards will result in disciplinary action including possible termination of employment, dismissal from one's board or volunteer duties, and possible civil or criminal prosecution if warranted.

Definitions

Employee: Means any individual appointed or hired by the Senior Pastor, or elected by the church body, as an employee, board member, consultant, or volunteer for purposes of serving in the Ministry.

Fraudulent, Dishonest or Improper Conduct: Means a deliberate act or failure to act with the intention of obtaining an unauthorized benefit. Examples of such conduct include, but are not limited to the following:

- forgery or alteration of documents;

- unauthorized alteration or manipulation of computer files;
- fraudulent financial reporting;
- pursuit of a benefit or advantage in violation of the Ministry's *Conflict of Interest Policy*;
- misappropriation or misuse of the Ministry's resources, such as funds, supplies, or other assets;
- authorizing or receiving compensation for goods not received or services not performed;
- authorizing or receiving compensation for hours not worked; and
- any activity by a Ministry employee that is undertaken in the performance of the employee's official duties, whether or not that action is within the scope of his or her employment, and that (1) is in violation of any state or federal law or regulation, including, but not limited to, corruption, malfeasance, bribery, theft of Ministry property, fraudulent claims, fraud, coercion, conversion, malicious prosecution, misuse of Ministry property, or willful omission to perform duty, or (2) is economically wasteful, or involves gross misconduct, incompetency, or inefficiency.

Illegal Order: Means any directive to violate or assist in violating a federal, state, or local law, rule, or regulation or any order to work or cause others to work in conditions that would unreasonably threaten the health or safety of employees or the public.

Baseless Allegations: Means allegations made with reckless disregard for their truth or falsity. People making such allegations may be subject to disciplinary action by the Ministry, legal claims by individuals accused of such conduct, or both.

Whistle-Blower: Means an employee, board member, consultant, or volunteer who informs the Senior Pastor, Leadership Team Member, or the Chairman of the Church Audit Committee, about an activity relating to the Ministry which that person believes to be fraudulent, dishonest, or improper.

Rights and Responsibilities (Procedures)

Whistle-Blowers: Employees, board members, consultants, and volunteers are encouraged to report suspected fraudulent or dishonest conduct (i.e., to act as "whistle-blowers") pursuant to the procedures set forth below.

Leadership Team Member: Leadership Team Members are required to report suspected fraudulent or dishonest conduct to the Senior Pastor, Financial Administrator, or the Chairman of the Church Audit Committee.

Reasonable care should be taken in dealing with suspected misconduct to avoid:

- baseless allegations;
- premature notice to persons suspected of misconduct and/or disclosure of suspected misconduct to others not involved with the investigation; and
- violations of a person's rights under law.

Due to the important yet sensitive nature of the suspected violations, effective professional follow-up is critical. Leadership Team Members, while appropriately concerned about "getting to the bottom" of such issues should not, in any circumstances, perform any investigative or other follow up steps on their own.

Accordingly, a Leadership Team Member who becomes aware of suspected misconduct:

- Should not contact the person suspected to further investigate the matter or demand restitution;
- Should not discuss the case with attorneys, the media, or anyone other than the Senior Pastor, Financial Administrator, or the Chairman of the Church Audit Committee; and
- Should not report the case to an authorized law enforcement officer without first discussing the case with the Senior Pastor, Financial Administrator, or the Chairman of the Church Audit Committee.

Investigative Bodies: All relevant matters, including suspected but unproved matters, will be reviewed and analyzed, with documentation of the receipt, retention, investigation, and treatment of the complaint. Appropriate corrective action will be taken, if necessary, and findings will be communicated back to the reporting person (whistle-blower) and his or her Leadership Team Member. Investigations may warrant investigation by an independent person such as auditors, attorneys, or both.

Whistle-Blower Protection

The Ministry will protect whistle-blowers as defined below.

1. The Ministry will use its best efforts to protect whistle-blowers against retaliation. Whistle-blowing complaints will be handled with sensitivity, discretion, and confidentiality to the extent allowed by the circumstances and the law. Generally this means that whistle-blower complaints will only be shared with those

who have a need to know so that the Ministry can conduct an effective investigation, determine what action to take based on the results of any such investigation and, in appropriate cases, with law enforcement personnel. (Should disciplinary or legal action be taken against a person or persons as a result of a whistle-blower complaint, such persons may also have the right to know the identity of the whistle-blower.)

2. Employees, board members, consultants, or volunteers of the Ministry shall not retaliate against a whistle-blower who, in good faith, informs the Senior Pastor, Leadership Team Member, or the Chairman of the Church Audit Committee about an illegal order or an activity believed to be fraudulent, dishonest, or improper with the intent or effect of adversely affecting the terms or conditions of the whistle-blower's employment, including but not limited to, threats of physical harm, loss of job, punitive work assignments, or impact on salary or fees. Whistle-blowers who believe that they have been retaliated against may file a written complaint with the Senior Pastor, Leadership Team Member, or the Chairman of the Church Audit Committee. Any complaint of retaliation will be promptly investigated and appropriate corrective measures taken if allegations of retaliation are substantiated. This protection from retaliation is not intended to prohibit Leadership Team Members from taking action, including disciplinary action, in the usual scope of their duties and based on valid performance-related factors.

3. Whistle-blowers must be cautious to avoid baseless allegations (as described earlier in the definitions section of this policy).

Scripture Index

1 Samuel

14:6 144

2 Chronicles

7:14 94

Psalms

85:6 163
139:23–24 67

Proverbs

4:23 85
18:13 137
22:1 5
22:24 72

Ecclesiastes

10:12 139

Matthew

5:11 9
5:13 61
5:16 10
16:18 . . . . 27, 184
18 79
18:6 65
19:13–14 65
22:21 25
23:1–4 84
23:23 85
28:18–20 152
28:19 25

Mark

16:15 152

John

1:14 70
9:4 154
15:5 26
15:8 157
15:16 158
15:18–31 10
17:17 25

Acts

1:8 . . . . 27, 152
2:38–43 25
2:42 46
5:29–31 25
6:1–7 25
8 27
8:36–38 25
11:26 13
13 162
13:1 161
13–14 25
14:27 144
15:1 119
17:11 25
18:11 28
20:19–30 25
20:28–31 28

Romans

1:8 27

6:1–6 25
10:9–17 25
12:2 101
13:1–4 . . . . 25, 80
13:3 66
13:3–4 65
13:14 85
14 . . . . 101–132, 180, 192
14:1–4 106
14:1–23 25
14:5 109
14:6 113
14:10 108
14:10–12 112
14:13 113
14:16–19 116
14:17 106
14:23 109

1 Corinthians

1:12 50
3 82
3:3–5 50
3:4 82
5 63
6 79
8 102–132
8:13 116
10:12 71
11:23–26 25
14:33 172
15:10 92

2 Corinthians

3:18 91
5:7 110
5:10 108
5:20 152
6:14 26
8:6–8 91
9:8 77
10:4 26
10:12 80
10:17 86
12:9 91

Galatians

2:16–21 119
5:13 113
6:1–2 79

Ephesians

1:6 93
1:22–23 25
2:2 107
2:8–9 91
3:21 183
4:15 61
5:15 . . . . 69, 195
5:23 30
6:24 142

Philippians

1:1 25
1:9–10 58
1:27 119

2:13 91
3:2 28
3:10–14 70
3:13–14 18

Colossians

1:6 27
1:18 . . . . 25, 30, 49
1:23 27
2:8 28
2:16 119
4:6 . . . . 91, 128

1 Thessalonians

1:8 27
2:4 163
2:11–12 28
4:14 152
5:19 64

1 Timothy

1:15 143
2:5–6 25
2:9 100
3 79
3:1–13 25
3:3 75
3:4–5 121
4:9 143
4:16 78
5:17 18
6:20 90

2 Timothy

1:7	172
2:2	28
2:11	143
2:15	89
2:16	90
3:5	61
3:10	77
3:16	25
4:2	90

Titus

1	79
1:6–9	25
2:1	140
2:5	100
3:8	121, 143

Hebrews

4:12	25, 89
4:14–16	25
11:6	110
12	74
12:15–16	74
13:9	123
13:12–13	52
13:17	121
13:18	163

James

1:19	137
1:20	73
3	74
3:14–16	51, 75
4:6	70, 72, 95

1 Peter

1:16	26, 104
2:5–10	25
2:7–8	171
2:9	102, 103
3:15	58, 67
5:1–4	25

2 Peter

1:20–21	25
2:1	61
2:3	61
2:18	59
3:16–18	28

1 John

2:15	83
4:1	62, 190

Jude

3	12, 43
16	58

PAUL CHAPPELL is the senior pastor of Lancaster Baptist Church and president of West Coast Baptist College in Lancaster, California. His biblical vision has led the church to become one of the most dynamic Baptist churches in the nation. His preaching is heard on Daily in the Word, a daily radio broadcast heard across America. Pastor Chappell has four children who are married and serving in Christian ministry. He has been married to his wife Terrie for over thirty years, and they have four married children and four grandchildren. His children are all serving in Christian ministry.

You can connect with Dr. Chappell through his blog, Twitter, and Facebook:

paulchappell.com
twitter.com/paulchappell
facebook.com/pastor.paul.chappell

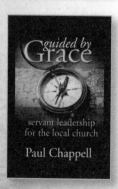

Visit us online

strivingtogether.com

wcbc.edu